i

How To Acquire Intellectual Integrity, Regardless of Your Race, Gender or Background

You Can Win the Respect of Others by Beautifying the World, No Matter Who You Are!

Glenn Arthur Fritsche

ISBN 978-0-9972042-5-4 (paperback)
ISBN 978-0-9972042-6-1 (e-book)

Published by:
The Enlightenment Press, L.L.C.
P.O. Box 421
Montevideo, Minnesota 56265

In appreciation for my parents,
Marie Magdalen and Arthur Leslie,
along with my aunts, uncles and cousins,
for their positive influence on my life

In the interest of maintaining gender neutrality, singular personal pronouns alternate in gender between feminine and masculine, section by section, throughout this text.

Table of Contents

Table of Tributes

(In Alphabetical Order by Last Name)

An Introduction to These Gallery Tours

Within each and every person are valuable aptitudes. These are gifts that all of us were born with, and they are the seeds of precious talents. With these talents we can beautify the world, each of us in our own unique way. However, these aptitudes must first be discovered, after which they then need to be groomed and developed into talents. For this to occur all of us need skillful teachers and mentors to guide us through life. As we then develop and employ our talents to beautify the world we become like artists and a wonderful thing happens: The people we encounter respect us for the beauty we contribute, regardless of our race, gender or background. This book is devoted to explaining these principles of life.

You may have heard the expression *making the complex simple.* While the concepts just described can at first appear somewhat baffling and perhaps unbelievable, they can be clarified and more easily understood through unique methods of explanation. In this book they are presented in the form of *word paintings* that are presented in a series of mental art galleries. You will discover that these word paintings make frequent use of analogy explanations that actually do make seemingly complex ideas easy to comprehend.

While your first reaction may be one of skepticism, this is to be expected. In spite of that skepticism, please be assured that you will find this book to be a source of both knowledge and enjoyment. Many may choose to read this book solely for entertainment purposes, assuming the concepts just described to be unrealistic and

1

perhaps even absurd. Again, this is to be expected. Please be assured that even if your sole motive is to be entertained, you are in good company with many others. You will not be disappointed!

In case you are curious, this book's cover image is symbolic of a couple dancing for joy with a new enthusiastic outlook on life and the world after encountering the concepts described in this text.

Having explained the above I now wish to introduce myself. My name is *Glenn* and it is my pleasure to be your guide. We are about to tour a number of intriguing mental art galleries, the likes of which you have not seen before. Enjoy!

An Introduction to Part 1 of these Gallery Tours

Underlying Life Philosophies

The Creators of the Universe intended Planet Earth to become a magnificent work of art. Therefore they created special Artists to prepare this planetary masterpiece. These created Artists are Bodies of Humanity. All of us were meant to be individual *cells* in various Bodies of Humanity whereby all of us would participate in beautifying this world. Through this artistic participation all of us can earn due respect from others in return for our contributions to beautify this world, each of us in our own unique ways. Unfortunately, something went wrong and a disease swept the planet, the disease of Selfishness. If this disease can be cured, there is still hope for this planet to be beautified and for all of us to earn the respect and appreciation we rightfully deserve. These concepts are further explained with the aid of the word paintings and analogies found in the art galleries of this first part.

It is to be noted that each of the galleries in this first series describes a basic principle of life and human nature, generally in simplified form. Together these basic principles provide a conceptual foundation upon which a structure of more complex ideas will be developed as we proceed through subsequent galleries. Your patience is kindly requested as you view the first few galleries because they may at first appear a little confusing. Please realize that you will soon see their relevance. At times it may appear that the concepts described in some galleries are unrelated to those of others. As such there will be various *twists and turns* along the pathway of ideas being presented. However, as we progress you will begin to see how seemingly unrelated concepts actually do combine to form a more advanced and deeper understanding of life and human nature.

Let us now begin this tour:

Gallery of Alternate World Views

Tour Guide's Introduction:

Two alternate views of the world are about to be presented. One of them you are already familiar with. The other is new to most of you and is certain to be intriguing.

> In this first word painting we see the summit of a tall mountain from which there is a view of the vast surrounding world. Reaching this summit is fairly easy thanks to an escalator that has been installed along the mountain's side. Anyone who wishes is free to ride the escalator upward to the top of this mountain and enjoy the views from its summit.
>
> On this summit, we see that two telescopes have been installed. Both of them enable visitors to view the vast surrounding world in close-up detail. There is a notable difference between them in that each has a different set of lenses. The first telescope with its unique lenses focuses only on certain areas of the surrounding world while other areas remain hazy and obscure. The second telescope with its unique lenses focuses on those other areas that were possibly obscured from the view of the first. Any interested person who visits this mountain summit can become fascinated with both of these telescopes, and the unique views that each provides.
>
> *(Continued on page 6)*

(Continued from page 5)

Nowhere on this summit is there any indication that the view from one telescope is superior to the other. It is apparent, however, that visitors are glad to have viewed the surrounding world though both telescopes, especially the second one with its unique set of lenses. That is because it provides an intriguing perspective, one which a great many have not seen before and is worthy of their consideration.

Interpretation:

The two telescopes in this word illustration represent two distinct views of the world. One of them is *your* present view, whatever that may be. The other is a unique view of the world as portrayed by the various gallery exhibits along this tour. Nowhere is there any suggestion that one view is superior to the other. Both views are uniquely interesting. Once again, people who view the world through the second telescope in addition to the first are glad they did.

As you tour this art gallery, consider that your present view of the world has been influenced by the people with whom you have lived and the circumstances that you have encountered. They have shaped your beliefs and your outlook on life and the world. Your life experiences have been unique and therefore your view of the world is unique. It is important to realize that virtually every person has a different view. One of the overall objectives of all these gallery tours is to master the *art of empathy* whereby one can then see the world from the many different perspectives of many different people.

Consider also during this tour that the exhibits in these galleries are intended to stimulate your thinking. Particularly as you proceed into the Gallery of Creation, you may find that certain paintings are controversial. It is not assumed that tour participants will agree with every concept that is presented in these galleries. Reactionary opinions of certain paintings will likely range from *pleasing and possible* to *ridiculous and absurd.* At the same time, if these paintings along with their interpretations stimulate thought and discussion, either positive or negative, they will have served their purpose.

Tour Guide's Commentary:

You may now be somewhat curious about the world views from that second telescope and why they may be controversial. The next two galleries provide beginning clarifications.

Gallery of Creation

Tour Guide's Introduction:

Our tour now proceeds into this Gallery of Creation in which certain mystery questions are addressed, namely "Who created this world?" and "Why?"

First Word Painting:

> In this illustration we see two Master Artists in the form of a woman and a man. Immediately in front of them is a large painter's canvas supported by an artist's easel. These two Artists are comfortably seated such that both of them can easily reach any portion of their canvas. Together they are busily creating a masterful work of art on their single canvas.
>
> Surprisingly, we also see that together with their easel and canvas they are suspended in space, in mid-air so to speak. There is nothing supporting them and nothing surrounding them. All we can see are two Master Artists in the form of a man and a woman, together with their easel and canvas, suspended in space, working together as a team, busily engaged with a masterful Creation.

9

Second Word Painting:

This is a view of the canvas upon which the two Master Artists that we saw in the previous painting are creating their Art. We see that this canvas is magical in that it has the qualities of a motion-picture screen. As we examine this screen we see that these two artists have the magical ability to create motion pictures instead of the usual still-life views that we are accustomed to seeing on most artists' canvases. We also see that with this creative screen our two artists can easily change focus anytime they wish. They can switch from an overall view of their entire artistic creation to individual views of specific areas. They can also focus in on the tiniest of details and give each of those details due creative attention.

Third Word Painting:

This is one of the views on our Master Artists' creative motion picture screen. What we see portrayed is the entire universe with its many galaxies, stars and planets, of which our Planet Earth is one small body amongst a huge multitude.

Fourth Word Painting:

> This is another view on our Master Artists' creative motion picture screen. While the previous view was of the entire Universe, this is a close-up view of Planet Earth, with its continents, oceans, prairies, forests, mountains, and waterways. It is a majestic view of astounding natural beauty. We notice something unique about this particular view. It is a depiction of this planet before it became inhabited with human beings. There are no signs of human life anywhere, no people, no buildings, no roadways, nothing of any human origin – only the earth itself. It is to be noted, however, that this view DOES include the presence of abundant plant and animal life, again in wondrous majestic beauty.

Fifth Word Painting:

> Here is another view on our Master Artists' creative motion picture screen, one that begins to stimulate our curiosity. On this creative screen we see a motion picture of a second artist team creating an image. We also see that this second team also has a motion picture screen upon which to create their art. In addition, we see that the image being created by this second team is also that of Planet Earth. In other words, we see that
>
> *(Continued on page 12)*

(Continued from page 11)

the Master Artists have created a picture of a second team of artists, and this second team is creating a motion picture of Planet Earth.

This description may at first be a little confusing. Hence, some additional clarification will be helpful. This painting on our gallery tour depicts a picture of a picture. First, we see a picture of our Master Artist team suspended in space with their magical screen. Second we can see the motion picture image on their screen. Third, we see that the image being created on their motion screen is that of a second artist team. Fourth, we see that this second team has a motion picture screen of their own for their creative work. Fifth, we see that the image being created by this second team on their screen is also that of Planet Earth.

Sixth Word Painting:

Here is still another view on our Master Artists' creative motion picture screen, one that further stimulates our curiosity. In the previous painting, on the Master Artists' motion picture screen, we saw an image of a second artist team creating an image of Planet Earth. In this painting, on the same Master Artists' creative motion picture screen, we see an image of many artist

(Continued on page 13)

(Continued from page 12)

teams, not just one. However, while there are many individual teams, all of them are jointly creating their images on the same motion picture screen. And, every one of these teams is in the form of a woman and a man. In other words, we see that the Master Artists have created a picture of many artist teams, and those many teams are all busy creating a single motion picture of Planet Earth on a single screen.

This description may also be a little confusing at first. Hence, some additional clarification will be helpful here as well. This painting on our gallery tour also depicts a picture of a picture. First, we see our Master Artist team suspended in space with their magical motion picture screen. Second we can see the picture being created on their screen. Third, we see that this picture is that of many artist teams jointly creating images on a single second motion picture screen. It is to be noted that each team does not have a screen of their own. Instead, they all share the same screen. Fourth, we see that the image being created by those many teams on their single screen is also that of Planet Earth. Fifth, we see that each of those many teams is focused on a different geographical area of this planet. Sixth, we can see the entire planet with all of those artist teams at work, with each team focused on a different geographical area. Seventh, each of those teams is in the form of a man and a woman.

Seventh Word Painting:

> With our curiosity aroused, we are drawn to this next painting which further stimulates our interest. In the previous painting we saw, on the Master Artists' motion picture screen, an image of many artist teams simultaneously working on a single painting of Planet Earth, with each team focused on a different geographical area. In this painting we are again viewing the Master Artists' motion picture screen, but now we see a close-up view of only one artist team, one among the many teams we saw in the previous painting. Once again, this single team is busy creating an image of a single geographical area of our planet. Like the others, this single team is also in the form of two bodies, those of a woman and a man.

Eighth Word Painting:

> In this painting, we see an even closer view of the artist team depicted in the previous painting. Here we see only the team itself, not the screen upon which they are creating their art. We again see the image of two bodies, those of a woman and a man. However, in this close-up view we also see that these two bodies are each made up of many individual *cells*. And, guess what? Each of these individual cells is an actual human being.

Interpretation:

We are surprised to see that this artist team shown in the *form* of two bodies is actually a collection of many individual human beings acting together as a group, or as a single body of humanity. This collective group of individual human beings is focused on a specific area of our planet. Whatever is being created in their specific area is the result of their joint creative effort.

We now give additional thought to the previous painting that depicted many artist teams, with each team focused on a specific area of the planet. We come to realize that, once again, each of these many teams is actually a large group of individual human beings acting together as a single group, or as a single body of humanity.

We may now come to the conclusion that there are many individual bodies of humanity on this planet, each consisting of a group of many individual human beings, with each group having its own artistic agenda.

Once again, this description may be a little confusing at first and some additional clarification may be helpful: The Master Artists depicted in the previous paintings are NOT actual human beings. Similarly, the artist teams shown in the motion picture paintings created by the Master Artists are NOT actual human beings either. However, each of the many *cells* within the bodies of those man and woman artist teams created by the Master Artists IS an actual human being.

A conclusion may now be drawn: Each and every person in this world is a *cell* in a body of humanity that has been created by the Master Artists.

15

Tour Guide's Commentary:

A question now comes to our minds: Are these bodies of humanity that function as artist teams creating good art, bad art, or some variation in between? The answer to this question will become apparent as we progress through the various gallery tours in this text.

Gallery of Despair

Tour Guide's Introduction:

You are about to discover that there are many "twists and turns" along our tours through this art gallery. The message to be conveyed in this section may be shocking to some. It may be contrary to many people's present ideas about life and the world, ideas that were formed during their childhood and adolescent training. For this section of our tour, participants are encouraged to temporarily suspend their previously formed beliefs, and give the message in this gallery some consideration. Admittedly, the ideas presented here will always be subject to debate, disagreement, and possibly ridicule. At the same time however, based upon the tangible evidence that we see in our surrounding world, these ideas do correlate with what is actually happening.

It is often said: "The road to misery is paved with good intentions." With regard to our personal lives, many of us can agree. This is because many of us have experienced personal frustrations as we have tried to fulfill our "good intentions." In this section of our gallery tour we are about to learn that the Master Artists who created our world have experienced similar frustrations.

First Word Painting:

In this painting we again see our two Master Artists. As in the original painting that we viewed at the start of this tour, we see them suspended in space with nothing surrounding them. All that we see are two Master Artists in the form of a woman and a man along with their magical screen upon which they are busily engaged with their many artistic Creations.

As we view these two Master Artists more closely we are astonished to see them "crying their eyes out." We see that they are as emotionally distraught as any human beings ever were, and even more so.

Interpretation:

When we see their exasperation and sorrow we wonder: What has happened? How can these two Master Artists with all their amazing abilities be so upset? What has gone wrong? As we proceed with our tour in this gallery, we will begin to understand the reasons for their frustration, exasperation and sorrow.

.

Second Word Painting:

In this next painting is a scene from long ago, millions or even billions of years ago, back to the time when the seeds of human life were first planted here on Planet Earth. In this scene we see our two Master Artists embarking upon a new creative artistic adventure.

You will recall the painting that we viewed earlier that depicted Planet Earth with a majestic array of plant and animal life, but with no form of human life or anything created by human beings.

In this painting we see that our two Master Artists have decided to create something entirely new and different. Their motive is that of pure artistic curiosity. **Instead of creating art forms directly, they have decided to instead create actual artists with the ability to independently create whatever they wish.** In addition, our Master Artists have decided to make Planet Earth the canvas upon which these created artists will express their artistic creativity.

Interpretation:

As it happens, for an artist to *really* be creative, he must have the freedom to create whatever he desires. To simply follow the directions of another is not being very creative. **To be a real artist one needs the *free will* to create whatever one believes to be truly magnificent.** With this realization, our two Master Artists created Bodies of Humanity with the *free will* to create whatever they desire here on Planet Earth.

Again, this artistic creation was a bold creative experiment on the part of our two Master Artists. Their presumption was that their created artists in the forms of various bodies of humanity would create real beauty. Our Master Artists expected to see their created artists enhance Planet Earth (which was already naturally beautiful) into an ever more wondrous and beautiful planet. Our Master Artists were anticipating enhanced beauty of nature, enhanced beauty of the environment, and wondrous harmony between individual artists.

What our two Master Artists did not anticipate is that *free will* would evolve into the DISEASE OF SELFISHNESS to the degree that it has. As a result we have disharmony, unrest, violence, pain, and suffering all across our planet. In addition, instead of enhancing our environment into an ever more beautiful creation, it is becoming defaced and ever more deplorable.

Since these two Master Artists have given their created human artists the *free will* to create whatever they please, these Master Artists are powerless to intervene. Instead, all they can do is observe with helpless agony what has actually happened. What was intended to be a wondrous artistic adventure for the creation of beauty has turned into a catastrophic disaster. Not only have their created bodies of humanity thoroughly defaced what was once a beautiful planet, they have also developed the means to completely destroy it, and possibly will. No wonder we saw our beloved Master Artists "crying their eyes out" in that previous painting!

Third Word Painting:

> In this painting we see multiple scenes of violence in many locations around our planet. We see scenes of conquest and oppression for reasons of greed. We also see scenes of defensive action for reasons of fear. In addition we see multiple scenes of revenge for what has happened in the past. As we view this painting we wonder about the reasons for all this conflict and war. We wonder why our wonderful planet has become the scene for all this violence, destruction, and despair. We wonder why it cannot instead be a scene of peace, harmony, tranquility and beauty.

Interpretation:

In this painting what we are actually seeing is a closer view of this *disease* called *selfishness.*

As we are about to see in subsequent paintings along this tour, **it is our basic human nature to desire equal value in return for what we contribute.** Our Master Artists assumed that we human beings would recognize this principle of equal exchange. They assumed that we would naturally strive to contribute equally in proportion to whatever we receive. Our Master Artists did not anticipate that so many human beings would strive to take advantage of others, by taking as much value as possible from others and by contributing as little value as possible in return. This inclination toward inequality has led to incredible resentment and complications all across our planet.

21

Another basic fact of human nature comes to light here. When negative value is imparted to another person or group, the natural response is to somehow, in some way, deliver negative value in return. This can lead to an ongoing cycle of injured people seeking revenge upon others, which in turn results in those others retaliating and seeking revenge in return.

There is much talk about so called *terrorists* and *terrorism*. Many if not most of these people are simply fighting back after being severely injured themselves, mentally and/or physically. Some of them have lost family members and loved ones through tragedies of war. Some have lost property. It is a natural human tendency for injured people (mentally and/or physically) to fight back in whatever way they know how. Sadly, certain ignorant individuals become "brain-washed" into believing that they will be rewarded with a luxurious afterlife if they will simply become a martyr for a cause. These supposed martyrs are nothing more than pawns who are being manipulated and controlled by more clever individuals with sinister desires for revenge, after having been injured themselves, mentally and/or physically.

Much has been written about the need to forgive others for their wrongdoing. This is extremely difficult for anyone to accomplish, especially while in a state of pain and suffering. Forgiveness may become easier for those whose level of consciousness has elevated to the point where they truly understand their fellow women and men. Along this line of thought, there is a familiar quotation with words to the effect of "forgive them, for they know not what they do." Whoever expressed those words apparently had a profound degree of human understanding. Unfortunately, all too few of us ever achieve such a state of mind, especially if we have been severely injured through acts of selfishness.

This *Disease of Selfishness* causes bodies of humanity everywhere to be fearful. Many bodies of humanity on this planet are fearful that some other body will strive to take advantage of them, steal from them, dominate them, and even completely control them. For that reason, major resources—human and material—are devoted to military oppression and defense. Those resources could instead be utilized for the beautification of our planet and to promote harmony between its inhabitants.

While our Master Artists had the intention for our bodies of humanity to exchange value and beauty, what has often resulted through the disease of selfishness is the exchange of havoc and harm instead. These Master Artists have come to realize that what was intended to become their *child of beauty* has turned into a *monster of despair* instead. What is even more frustrating for our Master Artists is to realize that they are powerless to intervene, thanks to the *free will* that they have bestowed upon humankind with the hope that it would instead be used to create an ever more beautiful planet. Again, it is therefore no wonder that we saw our Master Artists "crying their eyes out" in that previous painting.

Here is another interesting thought to consider: It is common for artists to begin a work of art, become disappointed with the result, and then decide to destroy it and start all over. The same thing could happen with our Master Artists' adventure with creating our world. However, in this case it will not be the Master Artists' desire for this to happen. Instead, it will be their *created artists* endowed with *free will* in the forms of *bodies of humanity* who may cause it to happen. The actual world that has been created by these bodies of humanity could self-destruct through nuclear war. Hence, what began with good intentions could instead become an artistic adventure gone awry. Let's hope that appropriate measures can still be taken to prevent that from happening!

Tour Guide's Commentary:

While the subject matter in this particular gallery is clearly depressing, *hope* and *optimism* are presented in subsequent galleries. The last thing that our Master Artists want is for us as a society is to "give up." Instead, we are expected to exercise our *free will* by searching for solutions that entail practicing the Golden Rule, and once found, by implementing those solutions.

Gallery of Ideals

Tour Guide's Introduction:

It is interesting to envision what our Master Artists had in mind when they embarked upon their *artistic adventure* to create human beings with the free will to create masterful works of art all around our planet. We can wonder about what our Master Artists were *hoping* for. What did they *envision* as possibilities?

Along these lines, we can wonder how our world would appear if all of society functioned as a coordinated whole to make this entire planet a wondrous work of art. Possibly, a world of universal physical beauty and one of universal harmony IS a worthwhile goal for us as a world society to pursue. Obviously, these are idealistic concepts that some may view as unrealistic. Nevertheless, they are interesting ideas to ponder. The paintings in this gallery offer suggestions for our consideration that are admittedly idealistic.

Presumably, many tour participants have an array of additional views that could rightfully be included in this gallery. The views to be presented are by no means all-inclusive.

First Word Painting:

> This painting depicts a world of order and harmony amongst its many people where everybody gets along with everybody else. Every person has a meaningful role in society. Every person has an appreciation for every other person and thereby is liked and appreciated by every other person in return.

Questions:

Might it become possible to achieve universal harmony amongst all people?

Might this be among the many ideals that our Master Artists were *hoping* for?

Second Word Painting:

> This painting depicts a world in which investments in universal education have first priority. Every person has the educational opportunity to develop her full potential and thereby become a valuable and appreciated member of society.

Question:

Might this universal concern for personal education and development be among the many ideals that our Master Artists were *hoping* for?

Third Word Painting:

> This painting depicts a world where there is universal concern for child care in all segments of society. Measures are taken to insure that every single child is properly loved, nourished, cared for, and guided in her personal growth and development processes to become a healthy individual with a wholesome and satisfying outlook on life.

Question:

Might this universal concern for child care and guidance be among the many ideals that our Master Artists were *hoping* for?

Fourth Word Painting:

> This painting depicts a world in which only a minimal investment or even no investment in military defense is needed. The entire world is at peace. All countries and segments of society interact harmoniously with sincere respect and concern for each other.

Question:

Might a peaceful, harmonious world be among the many ideals that our Master Artists were *hoping* for?

Fifth Word Painting:

> This painting depicts a scenic park with an array of lawns, trees, waterways, and gardens that are all carefully groomed and managed to enhance their natural beauty.

Questions:

Might it be possible to expand this careful grooming and management to enhance the natural beauty of nature all across our planet?

What would such a world be like?

Might this be among the many ideals that our Master Artists were *hoping* for?

Sixth Word Painting:

> This painting depicts a city in which all the buildings and physical structures have been designed to exhibit architectural splendor. This architectural beauty is seen all around the city: in the places of business, in the residential communities, and even in the industrial areas. The overall view of this city's exquisite building exteriors is suggestive of *civilization at its finest.*

Questions:

Might it be possible to expand this architectural splendor to encompass all buildings and physical structures that are constructed everywhere, all around the world?

What would such a world be like?

Might this be among the many ideals that our Master Artists were *hoping* for?

Seventh Word Painting:

> This painting depicts a natural habitat for plants and animals that is carefully managed to preserve and enhance the beauty of natural wildlife. Every possible effort is made to preserve every species and have it fill its rightful position within the balance of nature.

Questions:

Might it be possible to preserve and even expand natural habitats for our plant and animal kingdoms all across our planet for everyone to appreciate?

What would such a world be like?

Might this be among the many ideals that our Master Artists were *hoping* for?

Eighth Word Painting:

This painting depicts a network of carefully constructed roadways that are lined with the scenic beauty of nature. All along these roadways are various trees, grasses, shrubberies, and other plants that are native to given areas. All are groomed and cared for just as if they were located in a park or recreational area.

Questions:

Might it be possible to construct and enhance all the streets and roadways all around our planet such that they provide pleasing visual experiences for travelers in addition to being mere transportation routes?

What would such a world be like?

Might this be among the many ideals that our Master Artists were *hoping* for?

Ninth Word Painting:

> Similarly, this painting depicts another view of nature with an emphasis on waterways and bodies of water. Included are creeks, rivers, ponds, lakes, and oceans. What is especially pleasing in this view is that one can see into the depths of these waters thereby indicating that they are clean and pure.

Questions:

Might it be possible to rejuvenate the many bodies of water and their tributaries all around our planet so that they may be clean and pure again?

Might it also be possible to obtain a similar purity in the air that we breathe?

What would such a world be like?

Might these be among the many ideals that our Master Artists were *hoping* for?

Tour Guide's Commentary:

The paintings and questions raised in this gallery are obviously idealistic. They are intended to suggest direction and hope for the future. They present visions of what may someday be possible through the actions of a coordinated, smooth functioning society in which every person's talents are developed and in which every person is fulfilling a meaningful role. Obviously, many obstacles remain to be overcome for such ideals to become reality.

As mentioned in the introduction to this gallery, there are many additional idealistic views within the minds of tour participants that could also find a rightful place in this gallery.

Please note that the ideas expressed in this gallery will be expanded upon in more detailed form in subsequent galleries after additional characteristics of human nature have been presented.

Gallery of Humanity

Tour Guide's Introduction:

Once again, these gallery tours will take many "twists and turns" as we progress. We are about to embark on one of them in this Gallery of Humanity. The paintings in this gallery will illustrate once again that each and every person in the world is part of a larger whole, a *body of humanity*. In addition these paintings clarify that within this larger whole every individual is faced with a unique array of challenges.

First Word Painting:

In this painting we see a close-up view of the internal anatomy of a human body (it could be that of a man or a woman). This is the type of view one might find in a school textbook because it illustrates the many interior systems found within the human body. These include the circulatory system, muscular system, skeletal system, digestive system, nervous system, and all the rest. This painting also shows that each system is made up of many individual human cells. We can also see that these cells act in unison as coordinated teams. In doing so, through these cellular team efforts, each system performs a vital function within the human body.

Below this painting is its title: *The Human Body and its Internal Systems*

Interpretation:

As we view this illustration we can see that the many cells have certain similarities, and yet each has certain attributes that are unique to a certain system. As an example, one cell might be uniquely suited to participate in the circulatory system, another might be suited for the skeletal system, a third for participation in the nervous system, and so on through all the systems within the human body.

Of particular interest is the fact that each and every human cell *contributes value* to the body. This is because the system in which a certain cell participates is necessary for its body to function. In addition we can see that every human cell *receives value* from its human body in the form of nutrients that it needs to live and grow.

In essence, we can see that every human cell in the human body is engaged in an *exchange of value*. Every human cell gives value to the body by performing a function in a vital bodily system, and every human cell receives life-sustaining sustenance from the body in return. In essence, we see interdependence between individual cells and their respective human bodies. Cells need their respective bodies in order to survive and be healthy, and bodies need their many individual cells in order to function efficiently and well.

Second Word Painting:

Here is a view of a body of humanity as described in a previous gallery. This view focuses on the *systems* within this body, realizing that each of these systems is made up of many individual human beings.

Following is a partial listing of the systems that we see in this view:

- Systems for food provision
- Systems for education
- Systems for health care
- Systems for housing
- Systems for government
- Systems for communication
- Systems for recreation
- Systems for entertainment
- Systems for personal guidance
- Etc.

Below this word illustration is its title: *A Body of Humanity and its Internal Systems*

Interpretation:

As you can see, every system in this word illustration performs a certain function within its respective body of humanity. Each is dedicated to the fulfillment of a certain human need or desire. It is also to be noted that these systems are in continual interaction with each other. They depend upon each other to function properly.

As we look at these systems in detail we see that each is made up of many individual cells, and once again each cell is an actual human being. All of these human beings have certain similarities. And yet, each has certain attributes that enables him or her to function particularly well in a certain system.

Every human being contributes value to the system of which he or she is a part. And, every human being receives life-sustaining sustenance from his or her respective system in the forms of physical and mental nourishment. Hence, we see interdependence between human beings and bodies of humanity. Every person needs a body of humanity in which to survive and be healthy, and every body of humanity needs willing and able people in order to function efficiently and well.

As we view this painting we become curious to learn more about those *certain attributes that enable a person to function particularly well in some systems but possibly not in other systems*. A *clue* to this answer lies in a person's natural aptitudes. They will be described in more detail later on this tour.

Third Word Painting:

> In this painting we again see an illustration of a body of humanity. Again we see that it is made up of many cells and each cell is an actual human being. What we also see in this illustration is that there are many *connections* between these human beings. It becomes apparent to us that through these connections all of these many people function together as coordinated systems. We thus become curious to learn more about these connections, their purpose and function.

Interpretation:

As it happens, the purpose of every connection between any two individuals is to in some way serve a personal need. It is with those people that one *exchanges value* of any kind that one has a *connection.*

Within certain geographic areas, people interact and function together through exchanges of physical value consisting of goods and services. Within these same areas (usually in smaller groups) people are socially connected with family and friends through exchanges of mental value in the forms of friendship and love. It thus becomes apparent that what binds individual people together into bodies of humanity is their need to exchange physical and mental value with each other: People need physical value to live in physical comfort. Similarly, people need various forms of mental value, including friendship and love, to experience emotional comfort and life satisfaction.

Here again is that view of those internal systems within a body of humanity that were briefly described previously. As we view the individual human beings within those various systems, two characteristics become apparent:

First, each of these human beings has certain *functional skills* that are unique to her or his position within the body of humanity, of which she or he is a part. For example, a doctor has specific skills that differ from those of a teacher, who in turn has specific skills that differ from those of a construction worker, and so on through all the many different career positions of society.

The second characteristic we notice is that these human beings have the ability interact with many other human beings and this entails the use of *communication skills*. In addition, we see that their ability to *effectively* communicate with each other is based upon their ability to *understand* each other.

Interpretation:

We can broadly interpret this painting to mean that every person needs to develop certain *functional* (career) skills to fulfill a meaningful position in society. In addition, every person needs to develop appropriate *communication* skills, and this entails acquiring an understanding of one's fellow human beings. Realistically, acquiring appropriate functional skills can at times be difficult. Similarly, learning how to understand others and to effectively communicate with them can also be difficult. Nevertheless, **this need for every individual everywhere to somehow develop those skills is among the many challenges our world society faces if we are ever to live in peace and harmony.**

Tour Guide's Commentary:

Techniques for the development of appropriate *functional and communication skills* will be addressed in greater detail as we proceed with our tours through subsequent galleries. Considering that the ability to effectively communicate with another person hinges upon one's ability to understand the person, two fundamental principles of human nature are about to be presented in the next two galleries.

Gallery of Value Visions

Tour Guide's Introduction:

In this Gallery of Value Visions our tour takes another of those "twists and turns." The fundamental message conveyed in this section is that each and every person has certain inner *value visions* that are of central importance in her life, and that an important key to understanding someone lies in determining what those value visions are.[1, 2, 3]

In this painting we see a Treasure Chest and its contents. It is filled with a collection of pictures—a great many of them. These are pictures of what people typically *value* in life. They depict what people *would like to have* in life, but not necessarily what they actually do have. Some people already possess these treasures. Others would like to possess these treasures and some day will. Others would also like to possess these treasures but will never manage to actually obtain them.

The pictures in this treasure chest depict the fulfillment of such basic physical needs as food, clothing, housing, and health care. They also depict the fulfillment of basic mental needs such as love, friendship, admiration, respect, and appreciation from others. In addition, they depict desirable living conditions, family relationships,

(Continued on page 42)

41

(Continued from page 41)

and social networks. For some individuals this treasure chest includes pictures of certain career positions they would someday like to fill, along with certain career accomplishments they would someday like to achieve.

As you might expect, there is also an array of pictures depicting material possessions, travels to exotic locations, and other life pleasures that many people would like to someday experience.

Interpretation:

Within the mind of every person is a treasure chest of values. Within this treasure chest are *visions* of what people would like to have and experience in life. These include visions of what people already possess and dearly treasure. They also include visions of what people would like to possess sooner or later in their lives. Some will be fortunate enough to someday see their visions materialize into actual realities. Others will never turn their visions into realities for a variety of reasons.

Some people focus their actions and energy on preserving what they already have and treasure. Some people engage in a plan of action to obtain certain treasures that they envision. Maybe their plans of action will be effective or maybe they will not; either way they are trying. Others would like to have a plan of action toward the attainment of certain treasures but lack the means to engage in one. Reasons could include a lack of knowledge, ability, qualifications, and/or financial resources. Others, as a matter of interest, may envision an effective plan of action but decide it is not worth their time or effort to implement it.

All this painting illustrates is that every person has an internal mental treasure chest of value visions—visions of what they consider to be desirable in life. As we ponder this fact we begin to realize that people become more understandable if we can determine what their value visions are, because those visions are the underlying motivators for their actions. Similarly, we also begin to realize that people will become even more understandable if we can determine what they are actually doing to materialize their treasured value visions, and also to maintain the treasures that they already have in life.

Tour Guide's Commentary:

During subsequent gallery tours these concepts will be expanded upon in greater detail.

Notes:

1. Frank G. Goble and Abraham Maslow, *The Third Force: The Psychology of Abraham Maslow*, (The Introduction is by Abraham Maslow, and the remainder of the book by Frank G. Goble.) Pocket Books (September 3, 1980), ISBN-10: 0671421743, ISBN-13: 978-0671421748

2. Milton Rokeach, *Beliefs, Attitudes and Values: A Theory of Organization and Change*, Jossey-Bass Inc Pub (June 1, 1968). ISBN-10: 087589013X, ISBN-13: 978-0875890135

3. Milton Rokeach, *The Nature of Human Values*, Free Press (August 1, 1973). ISBN-10: 0029267501, ISBN-13: 978-0029267509

Gallery of Value Exchanges and The Golden Rule

Tour Guide's Introduction:

In the previous two galleries, two concepts were conveyed: One is that every person has certain value visions that are of central importance in her life. The other is that each and every person is part of a larger whole, namely a body of humanity. In this gallery another basic principle of human nature is explained, namely that when people give something of value to others they expect to receive equal value in return.

A conclusion to be drawn after touring this gallery is that the best value exchanges are in the form of "win-win" transactions, and these are an exemplification of *The Golden Rule*, namely the desire to treat others as we ourselves wish to be treated.[1, 2]

Word Painting:

In this illustration is a depiction of smiling and frowning faces with a brief word description next to each as follows:

☺   ☺   Win-Win

☺   ☹   Win-Lose

☹   ☹   Lose-Lose

45

Interpretation:

This is a depiction of a particular mental characteristic that is inherent in human nature. It applies to *every* human being.

Just as we human beings have all been created with certain physical similarities, we all have certain mental similarities as well. Physically, we all have similar bodily structures even though each of us has a unique physical appearance. Mentally, we all have similar emotional structures even though each of has a unique personality.

To help us understand this mental characteristic that is inherent in our human nature, let's think of a situation where two people exchange something of value:

> If both are pleased with the exchange and believe they received something of equal value in return for what they contributed, this is a "win-win" emotional situation. Again, both are pleased with the outcome of this exchange.

> If one person is pleased with the exchange, but the other becomes displeased, this is a "win-lose" situation. The reason one may become displeased is because she may later decide that the value she contributed was worth more than the value she received in exchange.

> And of course, if both become displeased with the exchange for whatever reason, this is a "lose-lose" situation.

This human characteristic becomes easier to understand when we consider a few basic examples.

Let's suppose that one person gives emotional value to another in the form of a sincere compliment:

> If the other acknowledges this compliment by returning a sincere compliment to the original giver, both *feel* good. This is a win-win situation.

If the other appreciates the compliment and *feels* good as a result, but offers no acknowledgement or form of thanks in return, the original giver may *feel* a little hurt. This is a "win-lose" situation.

If the other misinterprets the compliment to be a sarcastic insult, and responds with a sharp criticism, both can wind up *feeling* hurt. This is a "lose-lose" situation.

Another example is in the form of a purchase where something of monetary value is provided in exchange for something else of monetary value:

Both parties can be pleased with the transaction, with each believing that she received something of fair value in exchange for what she contributed, a "win-win" situation.

Or, one party can be pleased while the other comes to believe that she was cheated and the transaction was unfair, a "win-lose" situation.

And of course, for some reason both can eventually become displeased resulting in a "lose-lose" situation.

Another common example is with an employment situation. An employee expects compensation that is equal to the value she contributes. The employer in turn expects to receive service from the employee that is equal in value to the compensation that the employer provides.

Sometimes a person will contribute to a charitable cause realizing that nothing of monetary value will ever be received in return. What this person does receive in return is *mental value* in the form of emotional satisfaction, realizing that she did a worthwhile deed. Sometimes this person will also receive additional emotional value in the form of positive recognition and approval from others for having made that donation.

It is to be noted that *mental value* is emotional in nature. Whenever a person *feels good* about something, she has received something of mental value that might also be termed *emotional value*.

In summary, people expect to receive equal value in return for what they contribute. This value can be in many forms—emotional or monetary. When people perceive that a value exchange was unequal, meaning they received less value in exchange for what they gave, they experience emotional dissatisfaction. This is a basic characteristic of human nature.

Tribute:

In appreciation for their inspiration and influence upon this writer, here is a brief tribute to Michael Doyle and David Straus:

★★★

Michael Doyle and David Straus are the authors of the book *How to Make Meetings Work, The New Interaction Method.*[1] Chapter 4 of this book is titled *How to Find Win/Win Solutions*.

The terminology and concepts of *Win/Win*, *Win/Lose* and *Lose/Lose* agreements are firmly embedded in today's culture and popular jargon. The question remains as to who originated them. The first written explanation that I have been able to find is in the above referenced text, the first version of which is a hardback edition with the copyright dated 1976.

At the time when that book was published, Michael Doyle and David Straus were principals of Interaction

(Continued on page 49)

★★★

(Continued from page 48)
Associates, Inc., a San Francisco consulting firm whose problem-solving skills included the training of people in their new method of making meetings work,

Another reference text is titled *Negotiation—Strategies for Mutual Gain, The Basic Seminar of the Harvard Program on Negotiation.*[2] The editor of this book is Lavinia Hall, and one of the contributors is David Straus in which he again describes these concepts in Section 3 titled *Facilitated Collaborative Problem Solving and Process Management.*

It is possible that another author or authors have described these same concepts in an earlier work. If anyone discovers such a description, it will be appreciated if you will please send an advisory note to the author's attention at the publisher's postal address provided at the front of this text.

Notes:

1. Michael Doyle and David Straus, *How to Make Meetings Work, The New Interaction Method.* Berkley Trade—Mass Market Paperback Reprint (September 1, 1993), ISBN-10: 0671224034, ISBN-13: 978-0671224035

2. Lavinia Hall, Editor, *Negotiation—Strategies for Mutual Gain, The Basic Seminar of the Harvard Program on Negotiation,* with Section 3 titled *Facilitated Collaborative Problem Solving and Process Management,* contributed by David Straus. Sage Publications Inc. (June 24, 1992), ISBN-10: 0803948506, ISBN-13: 978-0803948501

49

Gallery of Religions and
The Golden Rule

Tour Guide's Introduction:

In this gallery we are about to see that, in spite of many differences, all of the world's major religions agree on a certain fundamental principle of conduct, namely the *Golden Rule,* the principle of treating others as we ourselves wish to be treated. In other words, amongst the many different cultures of people around our world, at their hearts people are not as different as we might first think. Following in **alphabetical order** by religion are quotations from their respective texts, as compiled from the online encyclopedia *Wikipedia*:

Buddhism:

> *"Hurt not others in ways that you yourself would find hurtful."*
>> Buddhist Text Reference: Udanavarga 5:18

Christianity:

> *"Do to others what you want them to do to you."*
>> Christian Text Reference: The Bible,
>> Matthew 7:12

Confucianism:

> *"Never impose on others what you would not choose for yourself."*
>> Confucian Text Reference: Analects of
>> Confucius 15:23

Hinduism:

"One should never do that to another which one regards as injurious to one's own self."

Hindu Text Reference: Anusasana Parva, Section CXIII, Verse 8

Islam:

"None of you [truly] believes until he wishes for his brother what he wishes for himself."

Islamic Text Reference:
An-Nawawi's Forty Hadiths - # 13

Judaism:

"You shall not take vengeance or bear a grudge against your kinsfolk. Love your neighbor as yourself."

Jewish Text Reference: The Torah,
Leviticus 19:18

Sikhism:

"The truly enlightened ones are those who neither incite fear in others nor fear anyone themselves."

Sikh Religious Text Reference: p.1427,
Slok, Guru Granth Sahib,
tr. Patwant Singh

Taoism:

"Regard your neighbor's gain as your own gain, and your neighbor's loss as your own loss."

Taoist Religious Text Reference:
T'ai Shang Kan Ying P'ien

Tour Guide's Commentary:

As a matter of interest, even agnostics and atheists would have a difficult time disagreeing with that listing of central religious beliefs.

Along these lines of common central beliefs that are at the heart of the world's major religions, it is worth considering that principles of equal value exchanges with win-win outcomes as emphasized throughout this text coincide with those basic religious beliefs.

Changing the subject somewhat but still relative to matters of religion, here is another analogy for consideration: Think of a lake or even an ocean in which there are many species of fish and other creatures. Their whole view of the world is what lies within their body of water. They have no concept or understanding of what exists outside of that body of water in which they reside. Similarly, the many animal species on this planet have only a minimal understanding of human consciousness. Human thought and activities for the most part are beyond their comprehensive ability. As a result, we remain forever mysterious and unknown to the animal kingdom. It is interesting to note that we *seem* to live in a world of ascending progression with ever more sophisticated states of existence. Therefore, the same dilemma that species with lower forms of consciousness face could exist for the human species as well. For all we know there may be higher forms of life that are beyond our human ability to comprehend. A classic example is the concept of *Angels* that is accepted by some religions and rejected by others. It is within our human nature to remain forever curious about the mysteries of our creative origin. Possibly we will never acquire the mental ability to truly understand our origin because the underlying *Truth* of our existence may be beyond the capabilities of human comprehension.

To the best of my knowledge the "Master Artists" analogies provided throughout this text are not found in any religion. They are however a useful metaphor for describing the Intelligence at the heart of our universe, realizing that somehow and in some way all of us were created for some mysterious reason. If any readers so wish, they can interpret these "Master Artists" to be nothing more than an analogy for describing an Entity that is beyond the realm of human comprehension. In other words, the concept of "Master Artists" as presented in this text is not one that is "cast in stone." If any readers so wish, they can modify those concepts to coincide more closely with their personal beliefs regarding the origins of life and the purposes for our existence.

Gallery of Inspiration

Tour Guide's Introduction:

In a few of the previous galleries we were presented with views of how an ideal world might appear. For such views to materialize, people will need to make the most of their lives by somehow growing and blossoming into all that they are capable of becoming. Natural questions thus arise regarding how this might be accomplished: From where will people acquire the *desire* to grow? What will motivate them to invest the necessary time and effort? What will be their source of Inspiration? How can they open their minds to receive the necessary Inspiration and thereby be filled with the *desire to develop their potential and grow into all that they are capable of becoming*? A suggested answer in example form is provided in this gallery.

First Word Painting:

In this painting we see an overview of a two-way audio-visual communication system. Two individuals are shown that are communicating with each other audibly and visually, with some possible distance between them. What connects them to each other is some form of electronic or optical transmission that is readily available with current technology. There is no indication in this painting as to the physical location of either individual. Either could be located virtually anywhere on this planet.

55

Interpretation:

The purpose for the preceding painting is to provide a conceptual introduction to this next one.

Second Word Painting:

In this painting we see three individuals:

One of them is a person who could be a man or a woman, a girl or a boy, comfortably seated alone in a quiet room. Let's suppose it is a man. He is engaged in silent meditation. Possibly he is journaling with some form of writing instrument, whereby he is writing down his thoughts as they appear. While in this state of quiet meditation, he is pondering over certain questions about his life, particularly in terms of how his life might be improved, how he can make the most of his life, and how he might best practice the *Golden Rule.*

The other two individuals are the two Master Artists in the forms of a man and a woman that were introduced earlier. It happens that they are intensely interested in the above person's inner meditative thoughts. It also happens that they are receiving his thought meditations loudly and clearly through a unique means of mental transmission. At their convenience, when and if they choose, they respond with appropriate thought images and word explanations for that person to ponder. These responses are mentally transmitted such that they spontaneously appear at appropriate times within the mind of that meditating person.

Interpretation:

What we see in this painting is that a dialog is taking place between the person engaged in meditation and the two Master Artists. The person is requesting advice on how he can make the most of his life and best apply the Golden Rule, and the Master Artists are providing answers.

We can surmise from this painting that if we have questions and need help, the Master Artists will be pleased that we thought enough of them to ask, and they will gladly respond. It is their wish for us to lead artistically pleasing lives in which all of us maximize our abilities and at the same time practice the Golden Rule.

It is to be noted that answers from the Master Artists may or may not be provided immediately. Sometimes there is a time lapse between when questions are raised and answers are received. One reason may be that the person may first need to grow and mature a little more before he will be capable of understanding the appropriate answers and applying them.

It is also to be noted that if a person's request is in some way a violation of the Golden Rule, the Master Artists may decide to remain silent, or provide an alternative unexpected answer as a result.

Also, it is to be remembered that all human beings are endowed with *free will*. If one unfortunately falls under the control of another individual who is unwilling to practice the Golden Rule and strives to take advantage of others, life can be difficult and sometimes painful. This is also a frustration for the Master Artists, and is one of the reasons why we saw them "crying their eyes out" in the Gallery of Despair. Never the less, when we request their help they will do their very best to help us escape painful situations. Particularly, if we request their help early enough, they will do their best to guide us along a pathway to avoid unnecessary pain and suffering.

Third Word Painting:

> In this painting we again see our two Master Artists. We also see a *potential communication line* between them and every single person on this planet. We also see that some of these lines are open and busy with active communication. However, we also see that a great many of these lines are closed with no communication occurring at all.

Interpretation:

What we see in this painting is that many people *could* avail themselves of personal guidance from the Master Artists but do not. We can thus wonder about the reasons. Possibly they include:

Some people are not aware of the Master Artists.

Some people may be aware of the Master Artists but do not have the meditation skills needed to make contact with them. (Sometimes people are first motivated to perfect these skills after experiencing a certain amount of pain and suffering in their lives.)

Some people would rather pursue what they personally believe to be their best self-interests without regard for the Golden Rule and without regard for fairness and the wellbeing of others. As a result, they could care less about what the Master Artists have to say. What they do not understand is that the Master Artists actually have each person's best interests in mind. What they also do not understand is that life could be considerably easier and more satisfying if they simply availed themselves of this Masterful Resource.

Tour Guide's Commentary:

What is alluded to in this gallery is that a phenomenal Source of Guidance IS available to each and every person in this world if he will simply request it.

It is to be noted, however, that because human beings are endowed with *free will,* some individuals do unfairly take advantage of others. The Master Artists are aware of these unfortunate situations and are sympathetic. They will still do the best they can to help people in unfortunate situations, realizing that there are certain constrictions imposed by the selfish *free will* of others. Once again, herein is one of the reasons why we saw the Master Artists crying their eyes out in frustration when we toured the Gallery of Despair. They were in a state of sympathetic grief and pain over the suffering being endured by certain individuals.

For any tour participants who would like additional information on how to more effectively interact with the Master Artists and obtain their assistance, various suggestions are offered in subsequent galleries along this tour.

HOW TO ACQUIRE INTELLECTUAL INTEGRITY

An Introduction to Part 2 of these Gallery Tours

Basic Life Considerations

As explained in Part I, the purpose of our lives is to participate as cells in various Bodies of Humanity, and the purpose of these Bodies is to beautify the world. All of us are uniquely qualified to do this once we discover the natural aptitudes that we were born with and develop them into artistic talents. Once we do this all of us can earn the admiration and respect from others that we deserve, regardless of our race, gender or background.

It is therefore our responsibility to search for and discover our inborn aptitudes and to develop them into unique artistic skills. To accomplish this, all of us need the careful guidance of skillful teachers, counselors and mentors.

It is the entire world's responsibility to make appropriate guidance available to each and every person on this planet. These concepts are further explained with the aid of the word paintings and analogies found in the mental art galleries of this second part.

HOW TO ACQUIRE INTELLECTUAL INTEGRITY

Gallery of Basic Needs

Tour Guide's Introduction:

In this section of our tour, in the form of simplified illustrations, we begin to define some of the basic characteristics that lie at the heart of every human being.

First Word Painting:

> This is a rather simplistic painting in which we see two homes. One is smaller in size and of basic simple architecture. The other is of a larger, more elaborate architecture. In each of these two homes resides a family. Both homes are well kept and neat in appearance. Both appear to be reasonably comfortable in which to live. We can also see people coming and going from these two homes and all of them appear to be smiling and content with their lives.

Interpretation:

This is a simple illustration of a basic characteristic of human nature, namely that people have a desire to live in physical comfort. For some, a simple dwelling and lifestyle is physically comfortable, and that is all they care for. For others, living in physical comfort entails a more luxurious, elaborate lifestyle.[1]

This is such a basic concept that one might question the need for a word painting illustration. As explained by the famous psycholo-

63

gist Abraham Maslow, within every person is a hierarchy of human needs in ascending priority. At the base of this hierarchy is a desire to live in physical comfort. For most people, this basic desire takes precedence over everything else in life. Once this need is fulfilled, a person's focus shifts to more advanced, complex needs.[1]

When learning to understand a person, it is helpful to consider this basic principle in terms of what her desired living conditions and surroundings may be, and especially how those desires motivate her courses of action to attain them.

As we ponder this painting, we come to a certain realization. To live in physical comfort, people must contribute something of monetary value in exchange for the goods and services that they need to live comfortably. They need to engage in equal value exchanges— physical (monetary) value in this case. A *challenge question* now arises: How can people acquire the monetary value that is needed for them to live comfortably? Again, as we proceed with our tour through subsequent galleries we will search for this answer.

Second Word Painting:

This is another rather simplistic painting in which we see two groups of people. One group is rather small and the other rather large. Within each of these two groups we see that everyone is smiling and they all appear to be enjoying each other's company. More specifically, we can see that all of them are personal friends and they value each other's approval and appreciation.

Interpretation:

This is an illustration of another basic characteristic of human nature, namely that people have a desire to live mentally (emotionally) pleasing lives. Some people have a small group of friends from whom they receive mental admiration and appreciation, and to whom they provide admiration and appreciation in return. Others have a larger group of friends from whom they receive favorable attention, and to whom they provide favorable attention in return. Whether we value a small group of friends or a larger group, all of us have a need for mental (emotional) approval and support. [1]

As with the previous painting this is also such a basic principle that one might question the need for a word painting illustration. Referring again to Abraham Maslow's proposed priority of human needs, every person also has a need for both self-esteem and esteem from others. Once a person's need to live in physical comfort is fulfilled, these esteem needs are next in ascending priority. [1]

When learning to understand a person, it is helpful to consider who specifically her friends are. Also, who are the people she would like to befriend? Whose approval and appreciation does she desire? Who are the people that she would most like to impress? It is helpful to consider that the people she would like to impress and the manner in which she chooses to do so will influence her life decisions and planned courses of action.

As we ponder this painting we also come to a certain realization. To receive the approval and support they need, people must offer similar mental approval and support in return. Here again they need to engage in equal value exchanges—mental (emotional) value in this case. This entails the use of certain abilities that are often referred to as "people skills." Another *challenge question* now arises: How do people acquire the skills needed to engage in successful human interaction? Once again, as we proceed with our tour we will search for this answer as well.

The intent in this gallery is to simply focus on those basic needs that lie at the heart of every person's motivations and desires. Knowing the physical surroundings in which a person lives along with her circle of friends reveals much about the life of a person. Similarly, an understanding of a person's career skills and people skills with which she contributes both monetary and emotional value to others and is thereby able to receive those same forms of value in return also reveals much about the life of a person.

Again, the purpose of the paintings in this gallery is to focus on those basic human needs that form the foundation of human ambitions. Certainly, people have many additional needs that are more complex. They stem from this basic foundation and will be discussed as we tour subsequent galleries.

Note:

1. Frank G. Goble and Abraham Maslow, *The Third Force: The Psychology of Abraham Maslow*, (The Introduction is by Abraham Maslow, and the remainder of the book by Frank G. Goble.) Pocket Books (September 3, 1980), ISBN-10: 0671421743, ISBN-13: 978-0671421748

Gallery of the Gardens

Tour Guide's Introduction:

Here comes another of those "twists and turns" as another life theme is explored in this gallery:

Each and every person's mind is in many respects a *mental garden.* It's ultimate beauty and productivity is a direct result of how it was nourished and cared for.[1] During one's growing years of childhood and adolescence, this nourishment and care is provided by parents, teachers, and significant others. In other words, one's personal mentality is in many respects shaped and formed by the mental gardeners who guided its growth during one's early formative years. As a matter of interest, these mental gardeners may have been attentive and admirably skilled, or they may have been inattentive and terribly inept. People's lives beyond childhood and adolescence are dramatically affected for better or worse by the mental gardeners who guided the growth of their minds, and by the abilities of those gardeners or lack thereof.

First Word Painting:

In this painting we see a garden, an especially beautiful one. Within this garden are arrays of plant life in attractive formations. There are manicured lawns, carefully groomed shrubbery and trees, and numerous flower arrangements. Interspersed with them are fountains,

(Continued on page 68)

67

(Continued from page 67)
sculptures and other artistic ornamentation that contribute to this garden's beauty. As we view the various trees, we notice with interest that many of them are bearing nutritious fruits of various different types. And, as we view the manicured lawns and carefully arranged flowers, we also notice with some degree of surprise that this garden is also interspersed with arrays of nutritious vegetables, also of many varieties.

Interpretation:

As we view this painting, we begin to wonder why the gardeners have chosen to include so many fruit and vegetable plants amongst the masterful artwork of lawns, shrubbery, sculptures, and other ornamentation. As we ponder this question we come to recognize that while this is a garden of beauty, it is also one of productivity. Not only is this an attractive garden, it is also meant to be a practical, productive one.

As we wonder about the meaning of this painting, we begin to see the correlation between the garden we see depicted in this painting and the garden of the human mind.

As we further view this painting, we find the artistic beauty of the garden to be mentally appealing. At the same time, with a somewhat *matter of fact business analysis,* we recognize that the fruits and vegetables within this garden have significant physical (monetary) value. We then begin to wonder, how does *monetary value* fit in with the concepts of *art* and *beauty*? A simplistic answer then comes to mind: Both are needed.

As we further contemplate the meaning of this painting with its exhibition of beauty and practicality, we are reminded that such a grand garden cannot possibly materialize without the planning, care, and guidance of a master gardener—or possibly that of several master gardeners working together in unison and harmony.

Second Word Painting:

> In this painting we see a bountiful harvest that has been obtained from various different gardens. We see an abundance of fruits and vegetables. We also see numerous arrangements of flowers. Surprisingly, we also see an array of sculptures and other works of art.

Interpretation:

The purpose of the preceding painting is to provide a conceptual introduction to this next one.

Third Word Painting:

> In this painting we see another bountiful harvest. This is a plentiful assortment of *skills* that has emerged from various different *mental gardens*. These are the skills of teachers, counselors, farmers, painters, doctors, designers, truck drivers, secretaries, scientists, nurses, governors, builders, janitors, entertainers, athletes, engineers, musicians, manufacturers, pilots, longshoremen, philosophers, and actors—to name only a few.

Interpretation:

As we view the assortment of skills in this painting we realize that only a few examples are provided from a series that could go on indefinitely.

We also see that all these skills have something in common. All of them are utilized to fulfill the *human needs of others*, of one type or another. It is also to be noted that some of the skills have obvious mental artistic value—those of actors, musicians, athletes, and entertainers for example. Other skills provide obvious physical monetary value—those of longshoremen, pilots, manufacturers, engineers, janitors, builders, governors, nurses, secretaries, truck drivers, doctors, farmers, and again the list goes on indefinitely.

Another realization that occurs to us is that a great many people have a diverse arrangement of skills with which they provide both mental (emotional) and physical (monetary) value to others. Not only do they have career skills, in various ways they also have the ability to express beauty, love and concern for others. In other words, their mental gardens are not only productive, they are also artistically beautiful.

As we view the previous two paintings we see a clearer view of the correlation between gardens of plant life and gardens of human capabilities. When viewing the gardens of plant life, we also notice a distinction between the soil in the garden with its potential for growth, and the actual plants that emerge from this soil. When viewing gardens of the human mind, we notice a distinction between their *potential* for development, and the *actual* capabilities (skills) that emerge from those mentalities.

As we give further thought to the correlation between conventional gardens and those of the human mind, we are again reminded of their origin. Conventional gardens with all of their beauty and bounty emerge under the care and guidance of master gardeners. Similarly, human capabilities with all of their beauty and practicality emerge through the care, encouragement and guidance of master mental gardeners.

Another thought now occurs to us. *The credit for whatever skills and capabilities that we may have is due in large part to the master mental gardeners who guided our growth, especially during our years of childhood and adolescence.* These include our parents, teachers, counselors and virtually anyone with whom we had significant contact during our early years.

We now have reason to view people with the realization that their capabilities in whatever form (or lack thereof) emerged under certain growth conditions that were prevalent during their years of childhood and adolescence. Also, we realize that their capabilities (or lack thereof) developed under the influence of whichever adults had *control* over their lives during those early years.

After viewing this painting and the above interpretations we can draw a final conclusion: Virtually every person in the world has developed into who and what she is under the guidance and influence of *others*. Or in other words, virtually every person in many respects is NOT the result of her own planning, but rather is the product of those individuals who happened to be her mental gardeners during her years of childhood and adolescence.

Fourth Word Painting:

> In this painting we see a single garden and a single gardener. The garden has a number of attractive plants. There are beautiful flower arrangements mixed among a number of productive fruit trees and rows of vegetables. At the same time, this garden has its share of problems. The flower arrangements could be improved upon. Some artistic ornamentation would help. The fruit trees need trimming. Additional vegetables would help to make it more productive. Weeds are growing in certain areas. The lawns are in need of water. Etc. Etc.
>
> In this same painting we also see a single gardener with a bewildered expression on her face. She has just recently been assigned to manage this garden, but was not in charge of its original design, planting or care. Now that this garden is under her care, she is wondering where to begin. Her challenge is in determining how to bring life, beauty, and productivity to this garden. She can see that this garden requires considerable work, and she is determined to do the best that she can to improve it with whatever resources she has.

Interpretation:

We can now think of a young adult, or maybe even an older adult. In essence, she is now becoming the gardener of her own mind. She can see how her mental development has largely been under the influence of others during her childhood and adolescent years. She can see where she has managed to develop certain skills that have both mental and physical value. She can also see where there are certain problems in her personal development. As a result, she realizes that there are certain skills that still need to be acquired, possibly through reading and practice, or possibly through additional education and job experience. In addition, she can see where it may be helpful to seek the advice of a qualified counselor, someone who can truly understand her and be willing to help. Somehow, one way or another, she is determined to make these improvements.

The realization we reach after viewing this painting is that sooner or later, especially during adulthood, we become the gardeners of our own minds. Eventually it becomes our responsibility to make whatever improvements we can to our personal mental gardens, no matter what may have happened to us in the past, no matter who originally shaped our mentalities, or why. As adults, we are challenged to "wake up" and do the best that we can to improve our mental gardens with whatever resources that we can find.

Another consideration is important here: Gardening can be fun! Once we get the knack of it, bringing our mental gardens to life with artistic and practical enhancements can be both satisfying and rewarding! ☺

Fifth Word Painting:

In this painting we see a group of diverse people first described in a previous painting, consisting of teachers, counselors, farmers, painters, doctors, designers, truck drivers, secretaries, scientists, nurses, governors, builders, janitors, entertainers, athletes, engineers, musicians, manufacturers, pilots, longshoremen, philosophers, actors, etc. As clarified previously, this series continues indefinitely.

Interpretation:

As we view this painting we begin to wonder. What are the ingredients for career satisfaction? While there are many separate ingredients, our focus here is on one of the key ingredients that is an inherent principle of human nature: every person has natural aptitudes and when a person is able to utilize her *natural aptitudes* on the job, career satisfaction becomes possible. And, when a person is not able to utilize her natural aptitudes on the job, career satisfaction becomes virtually impossible.[2, 3]

Here it is important to clarify the nature of aptitudes. They are the "seeds of talent." When and if a person's natural aptitudes are permitted to grow into skills, and when a person is able to apply those skills in her career, job satisfaction then becomes possible.

Tribute:

In appreciation for his inspiration and influence upon this writer, here is a brief tribute to James Allen:[1]

James Allen (1864-1912) was a British philosopher and author who wrote nineteen or more books during his lifetime, all of a philosophical nature. All of them are still in print. His most famous work is titled *As a Man Thinketh.*[1] In this book he extensively uses the analogy of how the human mind is a garden and how the fruits of this garden are the result of whatever is planted there. At the time of this composition additional information regarding his life and work can be found at the James Allen Library website - www.jamesallenlibrary.com.

Like Shakespeare, his books are all in what is known as the "public domain," meaning anyone is free to quote from his work without legal restriction. A couple notable quotes from his book *As a Man Thinketh* are as follows:

"As the plant springs from, and could not be without, the seed, so every act of man springs from the hidden seeds of thought, and could not have appeared without them."

"Act is the blossom of thought, and joy and suffering are its fruits; thus does a man garner in the sweet and bitter fruitage of his own husbandry."

One could go on and on with quotes from this book. It is certainly recommended reading for everyone.

Tour Guide's Commentary:

This next painting is very simple in appearance but at the same time is rather thought provoking. It might be titled *The Gardeners' Dilemma.*

Sixth Word Painting:

What we see in this painting is the beginning of a garden, which is nothing more than a bare plot of ground. Beneath the surface of this garden seeds have already been planted.

A team of gardeners has been assigned to care for this garden, but they are faced with an interesting dilemma. They know that this garden is already filled with seeds, but they don't know which kinds of seeds. In addition, they are not even sure who planted those seeds. While they would like this garden to grow into one of beauty and practicality, since they don't know which seeds have already been planted, they are puzzled as they try to determine how to properly care for this garden.

This same team of gardeners may be puzzled with another question: Is it wise to plant additional seeds in this garden, or should they do the best they can to nourish the seeds that have already been planted?

Interpretation:

As you have likely surmised, what we see here is the dilemma with which personal guides are often faced. Personal guides can be in the form of parents, teachers, counselors, and other significant individuals. They know that within the minds of children and students there are valuable aptitude seeds. These are seeds that have been pre-planted in the minds of infants upon entry into this world. A mental gardener's dilemma lies in the fact that these seeds differ from one person to the next. In addition, they remain dormant within a person's mind and first begin to grow when and if the right growing conditions are encountered. If the right conditions are not encountered, these seeds can lie dormant throughout a person's entire life. If only partially suitable growing conditions are encountered, these seeds may begin to grow into plants but never reach their full potential. Personal guides would sincerely like to aid in the growth of these aptitude seeds. However, they are faced with a two-fold dilemma: First, they somehow need to determine which aptitude seeds have been planted in a given person's mental garden. Second, once those seeds have been identified, determining how to properly nourish their growth and development into useful skills can be a major challenge.

It may be helpful to again clarify the nature of those skills that can emerge from properly guided mental gardens. These are the skills that will enable children and adolescents to someday experience life's enjoyments and satisfactions. It is with the deployment of these still-to-be-developed skills that children and adolescents will someday be enabled to express beauty and become productive members of society.

The gardeners' dilemma that we see in this painting can be summarized with the terminology of popular jargon: The good news is that every person enters this world with valuable aptitudes that are pre-planted within her mind, and these seeds have the potential to grow into valuable skills. The bad news is that these seeds may never grow into their full potential, and possibly will never begin to grow at all. They can only grow and develop into healthy useful skills through the care and guidance of masterful mental gardeners. Somehow these seeds first need to be discovered and identified. Then, somehow mental gardeners need to learn how to guide and nourish their growth.

As we ponder the meaning of this painting we begin to wonder: How can a person's natural aptitudes be discovered, especially during her adolescent years? Similarly, how can an adult discover her natural aptitudes if they were not found during her earlier years? In addition, how can someone obtain guidance in developing her natural aptitudes into valuable skills? Suggested answers are offered in the next gallery on this tour, which happens to include an audio-visual presentation.

Notes:

1. James Allen, *As A Man Thinketh*, This book is in the "public domain" and can thus be published without legal restriction—hence there are many publishers. www.jamesallenlibrary.com

2. Johnson O'Connor, *Understanding Your Aptitudes*, by the Writing Committee of the Johnson O'Connor Research Foundation, free download available from the foundation's website www.jocrf.org

3. Margaret E. Broadley, *Your Natural Gifts—How to recognize and develop them for success and self-fulfillment,* Epm Pubns Inc; 3rd edition (August 1, 1991), ISBN-10: 0939009560, ISBN-13: 978-0939009565.

Gallery of Personal Guidance

Tour Guide's Introduction:

In the previous gallery the concept of mental gardens was presented. In addition, the concept of having master gardeners available to nourish the growth of these gardens was emphasized. A conclusion to be drawn after touring the previous gallery is this: All of us need assistance with our personal development. Therefore, in this gallery the importance of finding proper personal guidance is emphasized.

An Audio-Visual Presentation (Not a Painting):

In this display we see two teenage students, a boy and girl, in the office of a career counselor. This display is unique. Instead of it being a painting it is actually an audiovisual display—a motion picture with a sound track. We can simply "push a button" at our convenience and the presentation will begin. As we do so, we are able to observe and listen to their discussion.

The two students are posing questions to their counselor along these lines:

Which careers should we seriously consider?

Which careers would we be good at?

Which careers would we enjoy?

(Continued on page 80)

(Continued from page 79)

How can we find the right careers that will provide us with life satisfaction?

The counselor in turn responds with recommendations along the following lines:

To properly answer your questions we first need to determine your natural aptitudes. Please be assured that you DO have them. They are unique *seeds* within your mind that you were born with. They CAN grow and develop into valuable skills. After these skills are developed, utilizing them in your future careers is ESSENTIAL for you to experience career satisfaction. Arrangements can be made for you to engage in a testing program that will reveal your natural aptitudes.[1,2,3]

Reference Information is available on a variety of different careers and the types of natural aptitudes that are needed to do well in those careers. After your natural aptitudes are determined through a testing program, you will be able to utilize that reference information to determine which careers are the best match for your unique array of aptitudes. When you do so, one or more of these careers will strike you as especially appealing. Based upon those careers that appeal to you, those

(Continued on page 81)

(Continued from page 80)

that will also entail the use of your natural aptitudes, you can then plan a pathway in that direction for career attainment.

Very likely, your pathway to satisfying career attainment will include some form of specialized education.

It will behoove you to find an experienced guide, possibly an older person, to help plan your career pathway and guide you along it. Perhaps you do not know of such a person right now. Still, with a little searching you can find one.

Please be assured that no matter how discouraged you may feel, no matter what problems you may have had, no matter what negative things anyone may have said to you, deep within your mind you HAVE valuable aptitudes. They are *hidden treasures* waiting to be discovered. Once you discover them through an appropriate testing program, with the proper guidance your aptitudes can grow into valuable skills. Simply stated, you HAVE potential. GO FOR IT!!!

Tribute:

In appreciation for their inspiration and influence upon this writer, here is a tribute to Johnson O'Connor and his friend Margaret E. Broadley who wrote a book about his work.

★★★

Johnson O'Connor (1891-1973) dedicated his life to researching and implementing the concepts of *aptitude discovery and development.* He is the founder of the Johnson O'Connor Research Foundation, which is still in existence today with offices in major cities around the United States. They have helped multitudes of people discover and implement pathways to satisfying careers based upon their natural in-born aptitudes.[1]

To this day this organization continues to offer aptitude testing and career counseling services to any person in search of advice. At the time of this composition, their website is www.jocrf.org. For many, the distance to their nearest office may be significant. Still, the service they offer is well worth the time, effort, and expense in terms of the lasting life satisfaction benefits that can be obtained from their recommendations. For anyone in an unsatisfying career situation and undecided about the type of career that would be more satisfying, the services of this organization are highly recommended.

A further description of Johnson O'Connor's work is provided in a book titled *Your Natural Gifts—How to recognize and develop them for success and self-fulfillment,* written by his friend Margaret E. Broadley.[2]

★★★

Another Tribute:

Here is a tribute to Linda Gale[3] and her book titled *Discover What You're Best At,* as well as other authors who have prepared similar texts.

★★

Realistically, a great many people do not have convenient access to a professional aptitude testing service like the one just described. Thankfully, a more "do-it-yourself" approach can be taken with the aid of certain books on this subject. As an example, one of them is titled *Discover What You're Best At,*[3] by Linda Gale. It contains a series of tests that one can self-administer to determine one's aptitudes. This same book also offers suggestions in regard to which careers require the use of them. One can then plan a life pathway toward such a career.

Through an internet search on popular book selling websites, similar texts can be found. It may be advantageous to utilize such a text with the aid of a qualified counselor, someone who is more familiar with various careers and suitable pathways to their attainment. However, if such a counselor is not available, one can still proceed alone by utilizing such a text as a guide. An obvious advantage with this approach is affordability. Such books in either new or pre-read form are generally quite inexpensive.

★★

HOW TO ACQUIRE INTELLECTUAL INTEGRITY

Tour Guide's Commentary:

This next painting is similar to one that we viewed earlier.

Here we again see the Master Artists and as a matter of interest we notice expressions of satisfaction on their faces. We are thus curious to know the reasons why. As we view their motion picture screen, we see a close-up view of a single artist team, one among the many teams that we saw in a previous painting. This single team is busy creating motion picture images on a single geographic area of our planet. Like the others, this single team is in the form of two bodies, those of a woman and a man.

This is also a close-up view in which we again see that those two bodies are made up of many individual systems of society. Each of those individual systems performs a specific function that fulfills a certain human need. Those needs are numerous and include everything from the physical needs for nutritious food and a comfortable home to the mental (emotional) needs for inspiration and love. Once again, each of those systems is made up of many individual *cells*. And again, each of those cells is an actual human being.

In this painting we also have a view of the geographic area on Planet Earth where this artist team, this body of humanity, is creating its artwork. As we examine this painting in greater detail we become impressed with

(Continued on page 85)

84

(Continued from page 84)

two particular qualities that stand out:

> The artistic creations in this artist team's geographic area of the planet are awesomely beautiful.

> The artistic team that is producing those beautiful creations is healthy. That is because the systems within their bodies, and the cells within those bodily systems are all functioning harmoniously together in marvelous coordination.

At this point for the sake of clarity it may be helpful to again consider the nature of those systems of society, examples of which include:

- Systems for food provision
- Systems for housing
- Systems for education
- Systems for health care
- Systems for government
- Systems for communication
- Systems for recreation and entertainment
- Systems for personal guidance
- Etc.

Interpretation:

There is a reason why these two bodies are able to produce artistic creations that are impressive and beautiful. That reason stems from the fact that the systems within these bodies, and the individual cells within their systems, are all functioning in harmony with marvelous coordination. We therefore wonder what the underlying secret may be to this amazing harmony and coordination. The realization then strikes us as an awakening experience: Every cell in these bodies is an actual person, and every person has amazingly managed to develop his natural aptitudes into useful skills. With the development of these skills, every person has found a natural position within a system within a body of humanity where his skills can be utilized. As a result, every person in these bodies is experiencing career satisfaction. Included in the many skills that each person possesses is the ability to harmoniously interact with the other people within his system within his body of humanity.

Tour Guide's Commentary:

Our reaction to the previous painting and its explanation may be that this is an idealistic situation, one that may be "too good to be possible." We naturally question if such magnificent artistic entities could ever materialize. This is to remain an open question as we continue with our tour. Our *hope* is to discover possibilities for society's advancement in this direction. Possibly we will find some encouragement as we proceed through the next area of thought in search for additional ideas.

Notes:

1. Johnson O'Connor, *Understanding Your Aptitudes*, by the Writing Committee of the Johnson O'Connor Research Foundation. At the time of this composition, a free download is available from the foundation's website www.jocrf.org

2. Margaret E. Broadley, *Your Natural Gifts—How to recognize and develop them for success and self-fulfillment,* Epm Pubns Inc; 3rd edition (August 1, 1991), ISBN-10: 0939009560, ISBN-13: 978-0939009565. (As explained on the foundation's website, Margaret Broadley was a personal friend of Johnson O'Connor. In this book she relates her ideas and perspective about his work and philosophy, as well as about aptitudes, careers, occupational patterns, and the importance of vocabulary.)

3. Linda Gale, *Discover What You're Best At,* Touchstone; 21st Revised ed. Edition (August 10, 1998), ISBN-10: 0684839563, ISBN-13: 978-0684839561

HOW TO ACQUIRE INTELLECTUAL INTEGRITY

Gallery of Mentors and Coaches

Tour Guide's Introduction:

We are now entering the Gallery of Mentors and Coaches. The previous galleries emphasize the need for qualified personal guidance and the associated benefits. This gallery comes to terms with the fact that for many individuals all around our planet such guidance is often unavailable. Ironically, for those most in need, such guidance is often least available. We are therefore curious to know how this dilemma might be resolved.

The suggested objective in this gallery is to somehow encourage the establishment of worldwide mentoring systems whereby every individual everywhere can have access to meaningful personal guidance. We would therefore like a better understanding of effective mentoring. We would like to know how mentoring systems might be developed and implemented on a grander scale. We would also like to know how they might become available to the financially disadvantaged, or in other words "free of charge." We are curious to know more about future possibilities.

While many questions will still remain unanswered, the forthcoming audiovisual presentation and paintings offer preliminary ideas. First will be suggestions for how mentoring systems might eventually be organized and appear in the future. Second will be suggestions for possible starting points in today's society from which more sophisticated mentoring systems might evolve.

It is to be emphasized that this gallery at best only offers partial views of possible solutions. Much still remains to be discovered. Various tour participants are likely to have additional insights and suggestions that would find a rightful place in this gallery.

An Audio Visual Presentation:

At this point along our tour, we encounter another audio-visual presentation rather than a painting. At our leisure we can "press a button" so to speak to begin this presentation and the following description begins:

For bodies of humanity to create real art in the form of internal harmony between people and the creation of external beauty all across their lands, each and every cell within those bodies needs to occupy a personally satisfying position in which she can contribute maximum value to her body of humanity and receive equal value in return. Unfortunately, it is extremely difficult for people to find and fulfill such personally satisfying positions unless they have the guidance of one or more capable mentors.

Mentors have an uncanny ability to recognize human potential. Generally, they are not discriminatory or prejudiced. Even if a person has had a hard time in life and demonstrates odd personality characteristics, astute mentors recognize that deep within that same person are valuable aptitudes, and those aptitudes are the seeds of talent. Not only do mentors have a profound ability to recognize another person's internal aptitudes, they also have great ideas regarding what it will take for those aptitudes to grow and blossom into useful life

(Continued on page 91)

(Continued from page 90)

skills.

While mentors can be in any age group and from virtually any walk of life, with a few exceptions they tend to share certain common characteristics:

Often they are members of older generations who have acquired considerable experience while traveling along the pathways of life.

Mentors are usually earning (or have already earned) enough physical (monetary) value to live comfortably, either in simple or more lavish surroundings. Since they are financially comfortable, they have time for the pursuit of mental (emotional) value. In fact, for them the attainment of mental (emotional) value often has a higher priority than physical value. As long as they have enough monetary value to live comfortably, that is all they care about.

Mentors have unique artistic abilities of their own. Those abilities enable them to be *Master Gardeners of the Mind.* Their artistic creations are in the form of human mentalities that they influence and guide. As they view the beauty of those mental gardens that they have nourished, influenced and cared for, mentors feel rich with personal satisfaction, a form of mental (emotional) value.

(Continued on page 92)

(Continued from page 91)
Throughout these mentoring systems there is a certain characteristic that serves to enhance their success. With their life-long accumulation of knowledge and many rich life experiences, mentors are *masters of empathy* and are thus able to truly understand the individuals that they counsel and guide.

And, guess what? Every association between a person in need and her mentoring guide is a unique mental *artistic adventure* all in itself! ☺

Tour Guide's Commentary:

We now arrive at another audio-visual presentation. This one is a documentary of a planning meeting. As we "press a button" to view this presentation, we observe the following:

Here we see a team of architects discussing their plans for a new structure. We see that there are an equal number of men and women on this team. Overall they appear to be intelligent and mature. From what we can tell, they represent a diversity of careers, culture, social status, race, and ethnicity.

As we focus in for a closer view, we notice that every person in this meeting has a printed booklet in front of

(Continued on page 93)

(Continued from page 92)

her. We are able to read the title of these booklets as it appears in bold type. The first line of this title is *Discussion Guide*. The second line is *Mentoring System Structure*. We thus come to realize that this is a team of architects engaged in a planning meeting for the creation of new mentoring systems. We also recognize that these meeting participants are primarily *system architects* as opposed to building architects.

Once again we come to the realization that Mentoring Systems in many areas of the world are largely undeveloped. They are still in *dream form* waiting to materialize. Considerable planning is still needed to determine how best to design, construct and implement these systems. Realizing the diversity of people in every culture, a diversity of planning input is needed.

As we view and listen to this group, the following issues and concerns are discussed:

> One of the challenges for any mentoring system to succeed pertains to the characteristics of our youth, particularly adolescents. How can they be motivated to participate, especially if they distrust the adult world and wish to assert their independence? How can they find the right mentors to advise them? These are still open-ended questions waiting to be answered.

> Mentoring systems for adolescents may include

(Continued on page 94)

(Continued from page 93)

aptitude testing, career advice, suggestions for wholesome personality development, suggestions for problem resolution, etc.

Certain adolescents have a natural independent streak whereby they are not likely to seek intelligent guidance from anyone, let alone follow it. However, those who are fiercely independent as adolescents may seek personal guidance later when they become adults, after they have made mistakes and endured personal suffering as a result. For them, a separate mentoring system that is geared toward helping adults get their life back on track may be a welcome solution.

A possibility for consideration is that of a dual mentoring program—one that is available to children and adolescents in the school systems, and another that is available to adults outside of the school systems.

Making mistakes is a natural part of growing up. The ability to recognize one's mistakes and seek appropriate guidance may first occur to a person after reaching twenty to thirty years of age, or maybe even later. Such individuals may also benefit from an aptitude testing program along with career counseling. However, they may also have personal problems that are especially difficult to

(Continued on page 95)

(Continued from page 94)

correct. Mentors who counsel young adults may recognize certain problems and sympathetically respond with statements like: "Yes, I have been through the same painful experiences that you have. I understand what happened to you and why. Here is how I finally grew out of those unfortunate circumstances:"

Another of the challenges pertains to potential mentors. How can they become interested? What will be their motivation to participate? What kind of training for mentorship is to be made available? What value will they derive from the program?

One of the key benefits for mentors may be the personal satisfaction associated with being able to help someone. That is because there is immense satisfaction in seeing another person's life grow and blossom into a healthy being under the influence of one's guidance.

Another of the benefits for mentors can be derived through training programs for mentors. These programs can provide opportunities for self-improvement at any age. Also, through participation in training programs, whether they are in the form of weekly classes or weekend seminars, there are opportunities for social interaction with other like-minded adults. Such interaction can provide

(Continued on page 96)

(Continued from page 95)
opportunities for new friendships. In essence, there is great potential for mental (emotional) value benefits through participation in organized mentorship training programs.

Many potential mentors may be retired citizens with extra time on their hands. Participation in a mentorship program could provide them with new interests and satisfactions in life.

Tour Guide's Commentary:

Clearly, in this world there is an abundance of inexperienced younger people with problems to solve. There is also an abundance of capable older people who have extra time to fill. Building the bridge between these two groups in the form of efficient mentoring systems will entail a series of planning meetings, as depicted in this presentation.

The seeds for these programs to be planted and the environments in which they can begin to grow are likely to be within our academic institutions. From there, mentorship programs have the potential to grow and expand into the broader surrounding communities and thereby become available to virtually everyone.

The previous two presentations in this gallery have offered suggestions for the future. Whether they are idealistic or realistic is a matter of personal opinion. Hopefully, they are realistic. Our tour now proceeds to a series of still-life paintings that depict basic ideas or concepts to serve as starting-points from which more sophisticated mentoring systems might evolve.

First Word Painting:

> This painting depicts a simple scene consisting of a neatly decorated room in which there are two comfortable chairs. Seated in these chairs are a younger and an older person. The expressions on their faces indicate that they are enjoying each other's company.

Interpretation:

We gather that this painting depicts a fundamental mentoring situation in which the younger person can benefit from the renditions and advice of an older person. However, we are unable to discern many details. We are unable to determine if this is a formal or informal setting. While we observe expressions of mutual interest on their faces, we are unable to determine the subject matter of their discussion.

Second Word Painting:

> This painting is a variation of the previous one in what appears to be a more formal professional environment. The room is possibly located in a school or office building. The older person is somewhat formally dressed and therefore appears to be a professional person. The younger person appears to be comfortable in this situation, possibly because the older person has been able to skillfully put the younger person at ease and initiate a friendship. From what we can see in this painting, they appear to be having a meaningful discussion.

97

Interpretation:

We gather that the older person in this painting is a professional counselor and the younger person is in need of a counselor's advice. The counselor possibly has significant expertise that has been acquired through both academic training and practical experience. The younger person may have sought the advice of the older person on her own accord, or at the direction of other significant adults. Possibly this younger person is faced with certain life problems and is in need of specific advice that the counselor is qualified to provide.

It is to be noted that since the counselor is a professional, somehow and in some way she will be in need of monetary compensation because counseling is her career and like everybody else she needs to earn a living. Possibly the funding for the counselor is provided through an organization such as a public or private school system. Or possibly, the younger person's family has the financial means to afford professional help.

It is also to be noted that not every young person has access to qualified professional counseling for a variety of reasons. One reason may be lack of availability, and another may be lack of financial resources. Again, it is often the most needy destitute poor children who are most in need of a mentor to help them.

Third Word Painting:

This painting is also a variation on the original in this series. The room in which the two are seated is more casual. Maybe it is within the confines of someone's private home. Maybe it is in a location where people meet for social reasons. Maybe it is in another location, possibly even in a restaurant. The older person appears to be a friendly mature individual. Since she is dressed in informal, relaxed attire, we are unable to tell if this person is a professional with academic training. Possibly she is not. Still, her facial expression and body posture exhibit the maturity one acquires in a life that has been filled with a variety of experiences, both pleasurable and painful. Simply put, she appears to be a person who knows a lot about life. The younger person could be any adolescent, girl or boy, from any background, privileged or underprivileged. She may be neatly or shabbily dressed. Her varied problems may be few or many, moderate or severe.

Interpretation:

This painting provides an example of an informal but valuable mentoring relationship that could take place outside of an academic institution. Based upon the relaxed body language and facial expressions that we see in this painting, we can imagine what might be the nature of their discussions. The older person may be reminiscing about her past, telling stories about various situations she encountered over the course of her life. The younger person appears to be enjoying those renditions in the same way she would enjoy any interesting story. We can gather that this discussion may have begun with the younger person sharing some of her current life problems. This sharing may have reminded the older person of similar situations that she encountered during the course of her life and how she managed to deal with them, possibly after considerable effort. Also, based upon the relaxed body language and facial expressions that we see in this painting, we can assume that there is a bond of confidentiality between these two. They feel free to be open with each other, realizing that whatever they discuss will remain personal and private between them. The younger person does not appear threatened. We gather that these two individuals appreciate and respect each other. We might assume that there is no exchange of monetary compensation. The senior person enjoys the emotional satisfaction of helping the younger person and appreciates the younger person's attention. This interaction makes her feel that her life is meaningful and worthwhile. The younger person appreciates the attention, love, care, understanding, and guidance that the older person is so willingly offering.

As we view this painting a natural question emerges. How can such a younger and older person come into contact with each other and form such a mutually satisfying bond? This question is the conceptual lead-in to the next painting.

Fourth Word Painting:

> In this painting we see a large group of diverse people, young and old, engaged in an enjoyable social activity. It depicts a situation where people of diverse backgrounds have a reason to interact and enjoy each other's company. This painting does not illustrate the location for this activity or the reason why this particular group of individuals are drawn together. This leads us to envision possibilities.

Interpretation:

Possibly, this is a gathering of people who are all part of the same religious community.

Possibly, this is a community that offers various social activities in which members can casually get to know each other. Who knows? Maybe they all dine together after their various meetings and services.

Possibly, this is a setting in which through normal conversation kind hearted seniors can informally make contact with both parents and children who have problems.

Possibly, enjoyable group activities can be arranged in which every participant is informally given due attention, encouragement and advice when and if needed.

Possibly, this is a community in which kind hearted leaders can introduce qualified kindhearted seniors to parents and children who have problems.

As one considers the possibilities for such group interaction, many challenges come to mind for which solutions still remain to be found.

Another problem of course is that a great many needy people are not affiliated with a caring organization that could help them if they were members. This is another problem that still remains to be solved.

Fifth Word Painting:

> In this painting we see another group of people. Possibly this is some type of fraternal organization that enables younger and older adults to socially interact. Friendships between the two can spontaneously occur because they all have a certain common interest. In these situations, senior members may be qualified to provide helpful career advice to younger members and be pleased to do so. However, it is well worth emphasizing that in these situations a younger member may first need to take the initiative to request the advice of a friendly elder before such a relationship can be established. Some encouragement may be needed.

Interpretation:

This particular group that we see gathered together in this painting may all share a certain common interest—athletic, intellectual, artistic, philosophical etc. This could also be a group of former military service members within which strong bonds often occur.

Of course, a great many people in distressful situations are isolated and lack the means or ability to become involved with a wholesome organization that can provide them with helpful social interaction. This is another problem that still remains to be solved.

Tour Guide's Commentary:

As explained in the Introduction to this Gallery of Mentors and Coaches, the exhibits presented at best offer partial suggestions for solutions. There are many obstacles to overcome. Much remains to be determined as to how adequate mentoring systems can be made available to the masses, especially those who are impoverished and most in need of help.

And of course, let's not forget the children who have been traumatized through acts of war, especially those who have lost family members and other loved ones. How can they be provided with adequate mentoring and resources to obtain meaningful starts in life that will lead to both career and social satisfactions? Or, in more alarming but real terms, how can they be deterred from becoming so called *terrorists* who understandably desire revenge for the harm that has been inflicted upon them, and instead be guided into meaningful, productive, pleasing lives?

HOW TO ACQUIRE INTELLECTUAL INTEGRITY

Gallery of Maximum Potential

Tour Guide's Introduction:

Our tour will now take another of those "twists and turns" as we enter this Gallery of Maximum Potential.

In an earlier gallery, the one of Creative Despair, we saw the Master Artists "crying their eyes" out. There we saw that what they had *hoped* would become an artistically beautiful planet, under the care and creativity of human artists endowed with free will, has instead become a place of continual human suffering resulting from the diseases of *greed and selfishness*. This leads us to wonder what these Artists actually had in mind. What were they *hoping* for? As we view the paintings in this gallery, we will ponder questions along these lines. In doing so, some of the concepts that were presented in the earlier galleries of Part 1, especially the *Gallery of Ideals*, will again come to mind.

First Word Painting:

> This painting is a reminder of those in the previous gallery. It is a rather simplistic painting in which we see a younger person receiving needed attention and devotion from an older person. This older person is a personal guide who is able and willing to help the younger one discover his natural aptitudes and develop them into useful skills.

Questions:

Might it someday be possible for every person everywhere to have such a capable, devoted personal guide?

Might it be possible to have a mentoring program in every country so that even those children who are born into the most disadvantaged situations have access to capable guidance to help them?

What would such a world be like?

Might this have been one of the *hopes* of our Master Artists?

Second Word Painting:

> This painting is another reminder of those shown in another previous gallery. It depicts an adult whose inborn aptitudes have been developed into useful career skills. With his array of skills he has been able to find a pathway to a desirable career position that he now fills, thereby giving his life meaning and satisfaction.

Questions:

Might it someday be possible for every person to have a careful assessment of the gifts he was born with, namely his natural aptitudes?

Might it someday be possible for every person to be guided into the formation of useful skills that utilize his natural aptitudes?

Might it someday therefore be possible for every person everywhere to attain a career position of optimum personal satisfaction?

What would such a world be like?

Might this have been another of those *hopes* that our Master Artists had in mind?

Third Word Painting:

> This painting depicts a person who has been guided in the development of communication and social skills. He thereby has the insight and ability to effectively interact with others in both career and social situations.

Questions:

Might it someday be possible to include in every school curriculum comprehensive training in the development of communication and social skills?

Might it someday therefore be possible for every person everywhere to acquire skills of effective communication?

Might it someday then be possible for every person to easily interact with others in family, social, educational, and career situations?

What would such a world be like?

Might this have been another of those *hopes* that our Master Artists had in mind?

Fourth Word Painting:

> This painting depicts a person who has the capability to contribute as much value as he desires to the other people in his world. The value that he contributes is both mental (emotional) and physical (monetary) in form. This person is also in the desirable situation where he is able to receive an equal amount of value from others in exchange for his contributions.

Questions:

Might it someday be possible for every person everywhere to effectively contribute significant and substantial value to others, both mental (emotional) and physical (monetary)?

Might it therefore someday be possible for everyone to live a life that is filled with "win-win" equal value exchanges in which he receives equal value from others in exchange for what he contributes?

What would such a world be like?

Might this have been another of those *hopes* that our Master Artists had in mind?

Fifth Word Painting:

> This painting is similar to the previous ones in that it depicts a person who is endowed with communication and social skills as just described. This person also has certain skills of *insight*: He has the ability to *see* which individuals are in need of certain values that he can offer them. He also has the ability to *see* which individuals can offer certain values to him in exchange, values for which he has a need. With his well-developed communication skills, he has the ability to make contact and negotiate equal exchanges of value with those individuals.

Questions:

Might it someday be possible for every person everywhere to possess such insight and communication skill?

What would such a world be like?

Might this have been another of those *hopes* that our Master Artists had in mind?

Tour Guide's Commentary:

Obviously, the previous paintings and their associated questions depict ideal situations. Still, it is helpful to see a meaningful purpose for our existence. It is helpful to have meaningful goals. It is helpful to have meaningful direction that brings satisfaction to our lives. The pursuit of maximum human development all around our planet can be a meaningful and satisfying goal for virtually every person to pursue.

Gallery of Theaters

Tour Guide's Introduction:

Referring to previous analogies along this tour, for a body of humanity to function efficiently the cells within this body need the ability to harmoniously interact with each other. For this to occur, they need to know how to communicate with each other. To efficiently communicate with another person one must have the ability to understand another person, and to understand another person one must be able to *see* the world from that person's perspective. This realization brings us to the concept of *empathy,* which is the ability to see the world from another person's point of view.

Many or most will agree that throughout our world, especially between differing cultures, people exhibit a remarkable INABILITY to understand each other, to such an extent that major conflicts often occur. It may be that **at the heart of world society's problems is a lack of empathic ability**. This is because when people do understand each other they are in a better position to search for and find mutually acceptable solutions to their problems, win-win solutions in other words.

A great many people stumble through life partially blind because they can only see the world from their personal perspective, but not that of others. For a gifted few, the ability to empathize comes naturally and it is these individuals who often emerge as leaders in our society through the use of this unique skill. If one is fortunate enough to have parents with empathic abilities one may then be fortunate enough to acquire similar skills through their example. For a less fortunate many in our society, empathic ability does not come easily. Many do not even understand the concept.

Empathy is a skill that is difficult to explain, let alone develop. However, such explanation and development does become easier with the use of certain analogies that are about to be presented in this gallery. Let's hope that this ability becomes easier to master for everyone once these analogies are understood.

Get ready! At this point, our tour of these galleries is about to take another of those infamous "twists and turns." This one will be MA-JOR. What you are about to encounter may be completely unlike anything that you have seen before!

First Word Painting:

In this painting is a scene of a typical movie theater in which there is a motion picture screen, an audio system, and many seats for occupants.

There is also a projector room in this theater in which an operator selects and projects various audio-visual recordings onto the screen and through the sound system. There is nothing unusual about this theater. It is quite like any movie theater that virtually any person might visit to experience a dramatic motion picture production.

Tour Guide's Commentary:

This preceding painting is the first of a sequence. We are not quite sure what to make it. We are therefore curious to proceed with this tour to see what comes next.

112

Second Word Painting:

In this painting is another scene of a movie theater. Unlike the one depicted in the previous painting, this theater IS rather unusual:

Within it are two separate motion picture screens instead of one, each with a dedicated sound system.

There are only two seats in this theater for the audience, instead of many as before. Even though there are two seats, only one of them is occupied.

There is also a projector room in which there is an operator. This operator selects the various audio-visual recordings to be seen on *one* of the two screens (not both) and heard through that one screen's dedicated sound system.

Whatever is seen on the second screen and heard through its dedicated sound system originates from another source.

In essence there are two separate audio-visual systems within this single theater. A dramatic motion picture production with sound effects can be playing on either of the two. The single occupant is able to see and hear both of them. However, the operator in the projector room only projects what is seen and heard through one of the two audio-visual systems.

As we examine the two audio-visual systems in this

(Continued on page 114)

(Continued from page 113)

single theater, we see that there may be a production playing in only the first system, or only in the second system, or in both simultaneously. The single occupant, once again, can see and hear whatever is playing on either or both at any time. He can easily shift his attention back and forth from one to the other.

Tour Guide's Commentary:

Again, this preceding painting is part of a sequence. We are not sure what to make of this one either. Once again, we are curious to proceed and see what comes next.

Third Word Painting:

In this painting is another scene of a movie theater. This theater is like the previous theater except with one MAJOR CHANGE. We now see that this entire theater is situated inside the head of a person.

Interpretation:

We now realize that this unique movie theater is actually a simplified depiction of the human mind. It is a *mental theater.* One of the screens with its dedicated sound system is focused on the outside world. On this screen, the occupant of this theater experiences the outside world through the five physical senses, especially those of seeing and hearing. The other screen with its dedicated sound system is focused on the inner world of thought. On this screen are portrayed the *images* of a person's thoughts. Through its dedicated sound system are heard the *words* of the occupant's thoughts.

Fourth Word Painting:

> In this painting there is a focus on that single occupant in the mental theater. We wonder: "Who is he or who is she?"

Interpretation:

As we ponder this question regarding who the single occupant in this theater might be, we can find the answer with the aid of a personal experiment, preferably when we are alone in a quiet place. We can close our eyes for a few minutes and allow our thoughts to drift wherever we please. As we do this, we will come to realize that even though our eyes are closed we can still see the pictures of our thoughts as they appear on our internal thought screen. Also, even when we disregard any and all external sounds, we can still hear the words of our thoughts through our internal thought sound system. Each of us can then wonder: "WHO IS THIS within me that is seeing the images of my thoughts and hearing the words of my thoughts?"

It now becomes clear as to who this single occupant is that we see in this mental theater painting. It is this same *being* within us that can see and hear the sights and sounds of our thoughts, as well as our surrounding outside world. This internal *being* has the name *Consciousness*.

Fifth Word Painting:

In this painting, there is an interior view of that projector room in the mental theater. Again, within this room is a different individual busily operating the audio-visual equipment that projects the sights of a person's thoughts onto the thought screen in the theater, along with the words of a person's thoughts through the associated sound system. As we look around this room we see stacks upon stacks of audio-visual recordings. We thus see that this is more than a mere projector room, it is also a library. We also see that the individual in this room is more than a mere operator of audio-visual equipment, he or she is also a librarian. (For ease of explanation let's assume this individual is a "he," although this individual could as easily be a "she." The same principles apply.) As a librarian, he not only operates the equipment, he also selects whichever audio-visual recordings are to be played at any moment of time.

As we focus more on this individual, we notice another interesting characteristic. Not only is he a librarian, he is also a modifier and a composer. He has the needed apparatus with which to independently modify and re-compose the audio-visual recordings in this library in any way that he prefers. As a result, the audio-visual recordings that he projects into the theater may be based upon previous recordings, but still differ significantly from the originals.

Interpretation:

As we view this painting, we cannot help but wonder about the person that we see is in this projector-library-composition room within this theater. We wonder "Who is he or who is she?"

This *being,* this librarian-composer that selects and often composes the audio-visual recordings to be played within a person's mental theater, has the name *Sub-consciousness.* He can be described as follows:

> He is a rather silent *being.* Even though he determines and often composes which thoughts are to be projected into our mental theaters, he remains largely a mystery. His reasoning processes are in a unique language all his own that remain below our conscious awareness.

> After this silent being decides which thoughts are to be projected into the theater, he translates these thoughts from his mysterious silent language into the *thinking language* that Consciousness understands. This thinking language might be French, Chinese, Swahili, Italian, Farsi, English, Yiddish, or whatever language a person's Consciousness uses for thinking and speaking purposes.

> Again, Sub-consciousness's actual reasoning and thinking processes lie below our conscious awareness and remain a mystery. Maybe they are of a visual nature, somewhat as we see in our dreams, but this is only conjecture.

> It is to be noted, however, that while operating beneath the level of conscious awareness, one's subconscious mind sees and hears everything that appears on the outer world screen and hears everything that enters through its associated sound system. In other words, whatever a person's Consciousness sees

117

and hears in the outer world is also seen, heard, and often recorded by a person's silent sub-consciousness.

Not only does one's subconscious mind see and hear the events occurring in the outside world, he makes independent judgments accordingly. Once again, these independent judgments are a major influence on whichever new thoughts he chooses to present for one's consciousness to see, hear and consider.

Medical science has proven that there are two hemispheres to the human brain, right and left. Whether the conscious and subconscious minds reside in separate hemispheres or partially in both is beyond the scope of this tour. Still, the fact remains that there are two specific reasoning areas within the human brain that are joined together by a channel of nerve fibers called the corpus callosum. This supports the idea that it is possible for a person to have two separate mentalities that work together as a team, namely the mentalities of Consciousness and Sub-consciousness.

Sixth Word Painting:

> This painting provides a close-up view of the thought screen in the mental theater that Consciousness is able to observe. In doing so, we observe one thought appearing after another.
>
> As we observe these various thoughts appearing on the screen we begin to wonder: "By what criteria does Sub-consciousness determine which recordings are to be played on this thought screen at any moment of time?"
>
> Similarly, we may also wonder "By what criteria does he decide to compose or recompose certain audio-visual recordings to be projected into this theater?"

Interpretation:

As explained with the previous painting, Sub-consciousness operates below the level of conscious awareness. He can best be understood in terms of the actual thoughts that he presents for Consciousness to consider.

Based upon the thoughts that we see projected into our mental theaters, we can draw certain conclusions about Sub-consciousness's *mode of operation*, namely the criteria by which he selects and often composes thoughts for Consciousness to consider. Remember the Gallery of Value Visions that we toured during Part 1 of our tour? The concepts presented in that gallery provide a clue. Sub-consciousness selects whichever thoughts that he *believes* are in a person's best interests at any given moment. These thoughts can be

119

basic and mundane, or they can be quite complex and sophisticated. These thoughts may be based upon valid reasoning and correct judgments. Or, these thoughts may be based upon faulty reasoning and erroneous judgments. A few basic examples are as follows:

"It is time to take a break and have a bite to eat."

"It is time to take a nap and rest a little."

"Let's call a friend and have an enjoyable chat."

"Let's engage in some form of entertainment."

"Let's focus on this work assignment that needs to be completed soon."

"Let's implement a plan of action to improve this situation."

"Let's proceed with this plan of action to obtain that which I desire."

"Let's figure out a way to *get even* and seek revenge for what has happened to me."

"Let's determine how to properly resolve this situation."

"Let's determine how best to *forgive* this person for what has happened, and move on with my life."

Etc. Etc.

As we can see from the above examples, a person's thoughts can shift from moment to moment. Sub-consciousness determines which thoughts he *believes* to be in a person's best interest at any given moment. This is not to imply that Sub-consciousness's *beliefs* are always correct. They may be based upon correct perceptions and sound judgment. Or, they may be based upon misperceptions and erroneous judgment. Either way, Sub-consciousness always selects whichever thoughts he *believes* to be in a person's best interests at any given moment.

There are many life-long memory recordings in this library. Sub-consciousness also makes *judgments* as to which memories are in Consciousness's best interest to consider at any given moment and projects them into the theater. These judgments may be wise or unwise. Sometimes these memory recordings are accurate, and sometimes they are garbled. When they are garbled, they are not exact renditions of what actually happened. Instead they may be quite different from the actual facts. Also, sometimes key memory recordings get misplaced and are no longer available when needed.

In summary, Sub-consciousness always projects whichever thoughts that he *believes* are in a person's best interests at any given moment and are therefore worthy of Consciousness's consideration. Sub-consciousness is susceptible to making mistakes. Sometimes he is right and sometimes wrong. As a result he can be responsible for either the right or wrong decisions made by Consciousness.

It is to be noted that while Sub-consciousness offers *thoughts* for consideration on the thought screen, Consciousness is the final decision maker in regard to actual courses of action that a person takes on the world stage. Similarly, Consciousness also decides upon the content of a person's verbal interaction with others, often in accord with Sub-consciousness's suggestions.

Seventh Word Painting:

This painting is a composite of several different thought screens, each of which is that of a different person. We notice with interest that some of the screens predominately depict pleasant invigorating thoughts, others predominately depict unpleasant thoughts, and still others focus mainly on stressful or even painful thoughts.

Interpretation:

As we view the several different thought screens depicted in this painting, we may wonder about the reasons for the significant differences in their thought content. We might wonder why does the Sub-consciousness of some people's minds project painful agonizing thoughts into their mental theaters while the Sub-consciousness in other people's minds projects pleasing happy thoughts? Possible explanations are as follows:

The thoughts that Sub-consciousness selects to be viewed in a person's theater are heavily influenced by past *emotional* experiences, and often may be reminders of those experiences. If a person has had the good fortune to have lived an enjoyable life, Sub-consciousness may select reminder thoughts of those experiences with the purpose of aiding a person in seeking and finding additional enjoyable experiences. Conversely, if a person has instead endured painful past experiences, Sub-consciousness may select reminder thoughts of those experiences with the *hope* that the person will thereby *avoid* such painful experiences in the future.

One of Sub-consciousness's silent *beliefs* is that a person deserves to live a comfortable life, and therefore *problems need to be resolved.* If a person has a certain problem, Sub-consciousness is apt to continually *remind* Consciousness of that problem with the *hope* that Consciousness will somehow find a solution with which to resolve it. Sub-consciousness might then present various ideas for Consciousness to consider, a few examples of which may be as follows:

A certain course of action to solve the problem

A certain person to consult with for advice on how to solve the problem.

An alternate course of action that alleviates the need to solve the problem.

Etc.

Again, the preceding are only a few examples among many alternative thoughts that may appear as a possible means to overcome a certain difficulty.

Admittedly, the preceding explanation may be overly simplistic. The Sub-conscious mind may be far more complicated and sophisticated than depicted here. Still, for the purposes of this tour, the preceding explanation provides a basic general understanding of its function.

Tour Guide's Commentary:

The following two paintings are a brief departure from the more general descriptions found in this gallery tour in that they pertain to unique situations that apply to certain people only. Since these unique situations are of interest to most people, and since they pertain to the Sub-conscious mind, they fit in well with the preceding discussion.

Eighth Word Painting:

In this painting we see the thought screens of people who through no fault of their own have fallen into virtually impossible situations. Their thought screens are filled with agonizing thoughts. Their Conscious and Sub-conscious minds have no available solutions to solve their problems and resolve the dilemmas into which life has placed them.

Interpretation:

As suggested in previous galleries, sometimes people find themselves in virtually impossible situations. Other individuals on the world stage have the *free will* to engage in selfish behavior, and some of these individuals are in *positions of power*. If one somehow falls under their control and becomes a victim of their behavior, life can become extremely difficult. As much as a person may wish to solve a certain problem, there might not be an available solution. This is one reason why we saw the Master Artists "crying their eyes out" in a previous painting. Because of mankind's *free will*, the Master Artists are not always able to intervene to correct unfair situations.

For people who find themselves in unfortunate distressful situations, sometimes what is known as the *Serenity Prayer* comes to mind, which in various forms reads somewhat as follows: "Please grant me the *ability to change* what I can change, and *the ability to accept* what I cannot change. Also, please grant me the *wisdom* to know the difference."

Sad to say, for some people life is unfair and their situations are beyond the ability of either their Consciousness or Sub-consciousness to correct.

Tour Guide's Commentary:

As a matter of interest, we live in a *balanced universe* which in popular jargon means "what goes around, comes around." As a result of this phenomena, every unfair situation that any person ever encounters will ultimately be resolved in a manner that is likely to astonish virtually everybody. Those resolutions, however, are the subject matter of another book, still to be written and published.

Ninth Word Painting:

In this painting is a daring view into the life records of certain world tyrants from the pages of history. None of them are living any more. These are not tyrants who inherited their positions from their parents, as when the thrown of power is passed along to a leader's heir. Instead we have a particular interest in those tyrants who rose from virtual obscurity to world positions of power in which they were able to control (and often destroy) multitudes of people. As we examine these records we look for *clues*. We wonder whatever happened to cause and enable them to acquire such power, to become such tyrants, and to inflict such cruelty on so many. As we search for these clues we come across an interesting detail. Most of those individuals have something in common: Most of them were the victims of severe child abuse.

Interpretation:

It may be *theorized* that during their childhood years, their sub-conscious minds were NOT able to realize that they are merely the unfortunate victims of abusive individuals, possibly their parents or significant others. Instead, it may be theorized that their sub-conscious minds became filled with a *fear* of the surrounding world. They may have seen themselves as victims of a cruel world over which they had no control. It may also be theorized that in an effort to resolve their suffering, to not be under someone else's con-trol again, and not have more pain inflicted upon them by the sur-rounding world, their sub-conscious minds contemplated thoughts of revenge by taking control of the surrounding world by any means possible. In addition, their sub-conscious minds may have plotted to use fear as a means of control, just as they were con-trolled through fearful methods during childhood. Also, it is con-ceivable that they did not care about any cruelty they inflicted upon the surrounding world, believing that they have already experienced their share of unjust cruelty from that surrounding world during their childhood, and it is time to seek revenge upon that surround-ing world. A conclusion to be drawn is that as a result of childhood abuse and emotional trauma, a person's thinking processes can be-come extremely warped.

It is to be emphasized that this interpretation is at best a theoretical opinion. This is a subject that may forever be open to debate, and for which many other plausible explanations are likely to be offered as well. Certainly, many abused children grow and mature into re-sponsible adults. However, as historical records indicate, under the right conditions abused children can grow into powerful tyrants and multitudes of people can suffer as a result.

Sadly, as we view the world of today, particularly in the areas of war and conflict, we see where many children are regularly subject-

126

ed to unfair abuse and suffering through the loss of homes, parents, and loved ones, along with ravages of hunger and disease. We can only wonder how they will respond as they grow into adulthood and strive to reconcile their pain and suffering upon the world that so unfairly abused them during their childhood.

Tour Guide's Commentary:

Now, after pausing for serious consideration of certain world dilemmas as described with the two preceding paintings, we will proceed with the normal course of this tour and the subject of empathy.

Tenth Word Painting:

> In this painting we again view the basic construction and facets of the mental theater. It is similar to the previous depictions of this theater, except for one change. As you may recall, there are two adjacent seats in this theater. One is occupied by the person's Consciousness, and the other is empty. In this painting we see that empty seat displayed in glowing color.

Interpretation:

We may now begin to wonder:

What is this all about?

Why is that empty seat displayed in such glowing color?

We may then begin to wonder:

What if my Consciousness could enter the mental theater of another person and occupy that empty seat?

What if my Consciousness could then see the two screens and hear the two sound systems within the mental movie theater of another person?

What if my Consciousness could see and hear the outer physical world in the same way that another person sees and hears it?

What if my Consciousness could also see and hear the inner thought world of another person?

As we ponder the above questions we come to a realization: This would be the ULTIMATE FORM OF EMPATHY. This would be the ideal way to truly see the world from another person's perspective, from right inside his mental theater, from the vantage point of that empty seat that we see depicted in glowing color in this painting.

One might assume that the outside world of another person appears the same to that person as it does to oneself. This is not necessarily true. It is important to consider that the focus of one person differs from that of another. As we endeavor to understand another person, it is helpful to know where that person's interests reside, what attracts his attention, namely what he focuses upon in the outside world. This can best be seen from that vacant seat within a person's mental theater.

With regard to a person's thought world, the images and sounds of another person's thoughts originate within the subconscious portion of his mind. As just explained, the nature of any person's subconscious mind is a subject all in itself. For now, realizing that a person's thoughts originate in his subconscious mind, we also realize that they can best be seen from that vacant seat within his mental theater.

In summary, *the purpose of this painting is to help us see and understand the concept of empathy in its ideal, purest form.* If the Consciousness within our minds had the ability to enter another person's mental theater, occupy that empty seat, and observe the sights and sounds of both the inner and outer worlds of that person, that would be the ultimate way to empathize with another person.

Eleventh Word Painting:

> In the previous painting that we just viewed there were seats for two occupants. One was occupied by the person's Consciousness and the other seat was empty, even though it was displayed in glowing color. This painting is similar, except for one change. This theater has only one seat, and it is occupied by the person's Consciousness. The empty seat that we saw displayed in glowing color in the previous painting has been removed. It is no longer there. It has vanished without a trace.

Interpretation:

The purpose of this painting is to help us come to terms with reality. The empty seat portrayed in that previous painting was helpful for explaining the concept of empathy, namely to put oneself in the position of another person's consciousness, and to see and hear the world (inner and outer) from that person's perspective. This painting clarifies that no such empty seat exists. Realistically, fortunately or unfortunately, it is not possible for anyone's consciousness to enter the mental theater of another person. Therefore, we are now confronted with these questions:

Is there another way to empathize with another person?

If we cannot view the inner world of another person directly, might there be an indirect way to do so?

The answers to these two questions are both "yes." They are explained in a sequence of paintings to follow.

Tour Guide's Commentary:

Warning! Here comes another of those "twists and turns!"

Twelfth Word Painting:

> In this painting we see two artists at work jointly creating a picture. As we look closer we see that they are NOT creating a still-life picture; instead, it is a motion picture. In addition, we see that they are simultaneously composing an accompanying *script* that is to be the sound track for this motion picture creation.

Tour Guide's Commentary:

Here again, we are not sure what to make of this painting. However, as we proceed with this tour it will soon be clarified.

Thirteenth Word Painting:

> In this painting we again see an illustration of the Mental Theater that we saw previously. Once again, the empty seat no longer exists. There is only a single seat with a single occupant, namely the person's consciousness. As before, we also see that mysterious projector room within which is that silent librarian and equipment operator, namely the person's sub-consciousness.
>
> In this particular painting we also see that this mental theater is portrayed as somewhat of a creative art studio. What we see here is that Consciousness and Sub-consciousness are functioning together as a team composing numerous dramatic audio-visual productions to satisfy their personal private viewing interests.
>
> As we look a little closer, we see that this team of Consciousness and Sub-consciousness is that same team of two artists that we saw in the previous painting.

Interpretation:

This occupant in the form of Consciousness and his companion in the form of Sub-consciousness are busy *envisioning* what it might be like to be seated within another person's mental theater.

In essence, we see that Consciousness and Sub-consciousness are attempting to be mental motion picture artists. As such, they are composing, producing, and directing mental motion pictures that depict the dramas of other people's lives to be seen and heard by only the two of them within their mental theater. Coming back to

131

the title of these gallery tours, namely this book, we can see that their mental motion picture composition efforts are *artistic adventures* all in themselves.

We now realize that this particular team of Consciousness and Sub-consciousness is implementing an *indirect method* for viewing the interior world of another person's mental theater. As such, they are *attempting* to empathize.

As we study this painting in more detail we also come to realize that just because they are *attempting* to visualize how the inner mental theater of another person might appear, this does NOT mean that they know what they are doing. Their perceptions may be right, wrong, or somewhere in between. To visualize how the world really appears to another person from within his mental theater requires the use of certain *skills*. For many, these skills are non-existent and remain to be developed.

Tour Guide's Commentary:

We are now at a point on our tour where we have a reasonable understanding of empathy as a concept. Also, we understand that to empathize requires the use of certain skills. However, we still don't know the nature of those skills or how they might be acquired.

Warning: Here comes another of those infamous "twists and turns!"

Fourteenth Word Painting:

In this painting we see another departure into the world of famous literature. Here we see the image of a detective and his assistant. We are reminded of Arthur Conan Doyle's famous characters, namely Sherlock Holmes and his invaluable assistant Dr. Watson. We are also reminded of the many other detectives found in both literature and real life.

Interpretation:

The thought now occurs to us that for a person to envision the interior world of another with some degree of accuracy, this person must have information to work with, information that is based upon actual facts. However, to obtain facts one must first discover the appropriate *clues* that can be utilized to determine those facts.

Another thought now occurs to us: Individual facts by themselves are mere *pieces to a puzzle.* One must also have the ability to put these pieces together into a meaningful picture to permit seeing what is actually happening, or has happened.

In summary, to determine what is occurring within the mental theater of another person and to thereby empathize with that person, one must be somewhat of a detective. One needs the ability to find clues, utilize those clues to determine facts, and then combine those facts into meaningful audio-visual motion pictures of what is happening or has happened in another person's life. As a matter of interest, once this ability is developed one is then in a good position to also predict what is likely to happen in another person's future.

Tour Guide's Commentary:

Having toured this Gallery of Theaters and having studied a theatrical model of the mind, we now have a reasonable concept of what *empathy* is, but not of how to develop actual *empathic abilities.* Thankfully, they can be acquired through a program of *empathy education,* which now leads us to Part 3.

An Introduction to Part 3
of these Gallery Tours

The World Chess Game Academy

As explained in Part I, our Creators intended Planet Earth to become a magnificent work of art. Their intent was for this artistic masterpiece to be produced by various Bodies of Humanity all across the planet, with all of us being *cells* in one or more of these Bodies. As *cells* we were intended to work as teams, with each team member contributing her artistic talents to beautify this planet in her unique way.

For real teamwork to take place, all of us need the ability to understand and effectively interact with the other members of our respective teams. Thankfully, there is a practical common sense approach to develop this interactive ability. It revolves around the ability to *empathize*, namely the ability to see life and the world from the perspective of those others with whom we interact.

Developing the ability to empathize entails acquiring an understanding of certain basic principles of human nature. These concepts are further explained with the aid of the word paintings and analogies found in the mental art galleries of this third part.

Gallery of the
World Chess Game Academy

Introduction

Tour Guide's Introduction:

Part 3 of these gallery tours is now focused upon the World Chess Game Academy. This is where basic principles of empathic reasoning are explained utilizing a series of easily understandable analogies.

Upon completion of our studies at this academy, we will proceed to Part 4 titled *Life as a Work of Art*. There, as the name indicates, it will be explained how the knowledge acquired at this academy can be applied to transform our lives into *true works of art*.

At this academy, two interesting analogies will be integrated together to provide a unique view of life and the world. The first is the famous Shakespearean analogy in which he describes the world as a stage and all of its many people as players on this stage. The second is that of how our world can also be viewed as a vast intricate chessboard, with each of its many inhabitants having a unique array of objectives, movement abilities, and game plans.

In terms of the Shakespearian analogy, we are sometimes members of the theater audience as we observe the performances of others enacting the dramas of their lives on the world stage without any participation on our part. As we observe them in action we can be pleasantly entertained by their performances, or we can have other emotional reactions, positive or negative. Similarly, there are other times when we are players on the world stage enacting the dramas of our lives while others are audience members who observe our performances without any participation on their part. As they observe us in action they can be pleasantly entertained by our performances, or they can also have other emotional reactions.

Likewise, in terms of the World Chess Game analogy, we are sometimes spectators as we observe others playing their unique chess games of life, doing the best that they can to implement successful strategies to win that which they desire. As spectators we can be intrigued with their skills and success, or we may be critical of their strategies and see needs for improvement. Similarly, there are times when we are busily engaged in our chess games of life, doing the best that we can to win that which we desire. There can then be others who are spectators that observe us in action. They can likewise be impressed with our skills and success, or they can also be critical of our strategies and see needs for improvement.

At this Academy there is a four-session curriculum:

> The first session is a more thorough explanation of the world stage and world chess game analogies. Here the *basics* of the game are explained in more detail to help provide a broader understanding of the entire curriculum.

> The second session focuses upon principles of human nature. With an understanding of these principles one can then more easily recognize an individual person's *movement abilities* on the world chessboard.

> The third session focuses upon *human strategies*, which in terms of chess game analogies is a study of *how* people play their games of life to win that which they desire, within the limits of their movement abilities. It is to be noted that as people engage in their life games on the world chessboard they are

simultaneously enacting the dramas of their lives on the world stage.

The fourth session focuses on the development of *detective skills* with which to interpret the underlying strategies that people are actually employing to win that which they desire. It is one thing to have an understanding of typical life strategies but it can be quite another to actually recognize the particular strategies that another person is implementing in her life. Specific skills are needed to enhance this recognition, and they are explained in this fourth session.

Finally and once again, *how* to apply the knowledge acquired at this Academy to improve one's own life is explained in Part 4 of these tours, titled *Life as a Work of Art.*

As we proceed with our studies at this academy, we will encounter some degree of repetition as some of the concepts outlined in this introduction are presented in more detail to further aid in understanding the more intricate concepts that follow.

As you are about to discover, this "Part 3—Gallery of the World Chess Game Academy" is rather lengthy and thus becomes somewhat of *a tour within a tour*, or if you prefer—*a book within a book.*

Let us now proceed with our gallery tour of this World Chess Game Academy. As before, you may expect the unexpected! ☺

Gallery of the
World Chess Game Academy

The First Session
Basic Introductory Concepts

Tour Guide's Introduction:

In this first session, basic introductory concepts are presented to provide a foundation for understanding the material to be presented in the remaining three sessions. You will encounter a limited degree of repetition as certain concepts are expanded upon that were first presented in the preceding introduction.

First Word Painting:

> This painting depicts a typical auditorium in which a dramatic performance is being presented. We see actors on the stage engaged in this performance. We also see a large theater audience observing and listening to the personal dramas being enacted on the stage.

Interpretation:

Throughout our lives we are both players on the world stage and members of the world theater audience. As we engage in our personal dramas of life we are the players. When we pause to observe and listen to the other players on world stage and consider their life dramas, we become members of the world theater audience.

Second Word Painting:

This painting presents those famous lines from William Shakespeare's play *As You Like It,* Act II, Scene VII:[1]

"All the world's a stage,
And all the men and women merely players;
They have their exits and their entrances,
And one man in his time plays many parts,"

Interpretation:

Once again, as so eloquently explained by one of world history's most famous writers, all of us are *players on the world stage.* All of us are involved in a multitude of personal life dramas as we seek to fulfill our personal desires, whatever they happen to be. Through this quest for personal fulfillment every person encounters a never-ending series of dramatic experiences. Depending on the situation, these experiences can range from very desirable to very undesirable. All of them are accompanied with emotional feelings that can range from very pleasurable to very painful, with numerous variations in between. Therefore, as we endeavor to empathize with others, we will be especially interested in their emotional expressions. We will recognize their expressions as important *clues* that provide insight to their underlying life dramas. For this reason, a description of basic human emotions will be provided in the second session of study at this Academy.

Third Word Painting:

In this painting we see a depiction of the conventional game of Chess. As we all know there are two players in this conventional game. The focus of this painting is on the basics of the game itself, which include the following:

a) Two Players

b) One chessboard

c) 64 positions on the board

d) Two sets of chess-people to move around the board, initially with sixteen individual chess-people in each set consisting of queens, kings, knights, rooks, bishops, and pawns.

e) Each chess-person has limited movement ability, with limited access to various positions.

f) Some chess-people have more movement ability than others, and therefore have access to more of the positions on the board.

g) Each set of chess-people is under the control of one player.

h) The basic game strategy is "win-lose" with each player determined to win at the other's expense.

Tour Guide's Commentary:

As you have possibly surmised, the purpose for the previous painting has been to provide a conceptual introduction to this next painting which is a little more complicated.

Fourth Word Painting:

In this painting we see a depiction of another game of
Chess. This one is more elaborate than the conventional game that we have just considered. Certain similarities with the conventional game are evident. However,
there are notable differences that cause us to wonder
what this particular game is really all about. Some of
this more elaborate game's characteristics are as follows:

a) Every person in the world is a player in this game.

b) There is a single chessboard, namely the world as a
whole. It is made up of many smaller chessboards
that are pieced together to comprise the larger
whole.

c) There are billions of positions on this world chess
board. Even the smaller chessboards have a great
many positions – tens, hundreds, thousands, even
millions.

d) In addition to billions of positions, there are also
billions of chess-people on this world board. And
again, even on the smaller chessboards the numbers

(Continued on page 145)

(Continued from page 144)

can be huge. Again – tens, hundreds, thousands, even millions.

e) Each chess-person has limited movement ability, with limited access to certain positions.

f) Some chess-people have more movement ability than others, and therefore have access to more positions on the board.

g) Unlike a conventional chess-game where the basic strategy is win-lose, that strategy does NOT apply in this world chess game. While many players do pursue win-lose strategies, it is actually win-win strategies that can be more successful when and if they are implemented properly.

Tour Guide's Commentary:

As you have also possibly surmised, the purpose for the previous two paintings has been to help establish a conceptual foundation for the remaining sessions of study at this Academy. As you will soon see, life chess game analogies are especially helpful for understanding and developing the skills of empathy.

For some, the thought of being engaged in a life game of chess may seem ridiculous, and even revolting. Few people envision themselves as participants in a game in which they are implementing various strategies to win. Similarly, few people utilize chess game terminology in their thinking processes. The purpose for the next painting is to address and hopefully reconcile those issues.

145

Fifth Word Painting:

In this painting we again see the Mental Theater of the mind. Again we see an internal thought screen and an outer world screen. Again we see Consciousness observing the inner world of thoughts on one screen and the outer world of activity on the other. And once again we see Sub-consciousness in the projector room flashing a series of thoughts onto the thought screen.

Interpretation:

It is to be noted that Consciousness can only see the thoughts that Sub-consciousness flashes onto the internal thought screen. Consciousness is unable to see or hear the reasoning processes that Sub-consciousness utilizes to determine which thoughts she will project onto this screen. Sub-consciousness utilizes a language and logic all of her own. This language and logic operates below the level of conscious awareness.

With regard to human mentalities in general, we are able to observe certain characteristics of human thought. One is that people naturally think about or envision *what they desire in life*—and this can be likened to thoughts about a certain desirable position on the world chessboard where they would actually have what they desire—a position that may be real or imaginary. People also think about *how* they can possibly achieve what they desire—and this can be likened to a *strategy* for attainment—one that may be realistic or unrealistic.

Once again, seldom do people think of themselves as being engaged in a life game of chess. Similarly, seldom do people utilize chess game terminology in their thinking processes. Instead, another language and another terminology is silently used within the realms of their subconscious minds, and again that silent form of reasoning takes place beneath their level of conscious awareness. What we do see are the results of subconscious reasoning and those results can be likened to the *plans of action* of a chess player striving to attain various desirable positions—namely a desirable state of mind and a desirable state of physical existence. It is to be noted that these desirable positions can vary widely between people. Some envision what they *believe* to be emotionally pleasing situations within humble physical surroundings. Others envision what they *believe* to be emotionally pleasing situations in the midst of vast material luxury. Some envision a pleasing life in the midst of a few close friends and family members. Others envision a pleasing life in the midst of a multitude of admirers.

In summary, people have many desires to be in pleasing life situations. These situations can be likened to positions on the world chessboard that they would like to reach. Whether they ever do or not is another matter.

Note:

1. William Shakespeare, *As You Like It,* Act II, Scene VII, This play is in the "public domain" and can thus be published without legal restriction—hence there are many publishers.

HOW TO ACQUIRE INTELLECTUAL INTEGRITY

Gallery of the World Chess Game Academy

The Second Session Principles of Human Nature

Tour Guide's Introduction:

As explained earlier, this second session focuses upon *principles of human nature.* With an understanding of these principles one can then more easily recognize a person's *movement abilities* on the world chessboard.

Value Visions A Basic Principle of Human Nature

Tour Guide's Commentary:

As you recall, earlier we toured the Gallery of Value Visions where it was explained that every person has certain inner visions of value. Since this is a basic principle of human nature it is also included in this section, this time with a shorter explanation.[1,2]

First Word Painting:

In this painting we see a treasure chest and its contents. It is filled with a collection of pictures that people envision within their minds—a great many of them. These are pictures of what people typically *value* in life. First and foremost they depict the fulfillment of basic physical needs such as food, clothing, housing, and health care. They also depict the fulfillment of basic emotional needs such as love, friendship, admiration, respect, and appreciation from others. Generally, these pictures depict desirable living conditions, family relationships, social networks, career situations, and so on.

Interpretation:

Again, all this painting illustrates is a basic principle of human nature, namely that every person has an internal mental treasure chest of *value visions*. These are visions of whatever he considers to be desirable in life. A more detailed explanation has already been provided in the Gallery of Value Visions.

Desirable versus Undesirable
The Underlying Principle of Human Emotion

Second Word Painting:

In this painting we see two side-by-side illustrations of a mountain. In each of these two illustrations we see an individual attempting to climb the mountain and reach its summit. As we look closer we see that each illustration is of the same mountain, and the same climber is shown in each illustration. There is only one difference between these two illustrations. In one, the climber is advancing upward toward the summit with a smile on his face. In the other, the climber is slipping downward away from the summit with a frown on his face.

Interpretation:

The summit of the mountain in these two side-by-side illustrations represents anything that a person might desire in life. It might be a pleasing emotional situation with family and friends. It might be a material or monetary goal. It could be any of a multitude of situations or things that any person might desire to experience sometime during his life. Whenever a person is able to make progress and advance toward that which he desires, he experiences pleasing emotions. This is represented by the smile on the person's face that we see advancing upward. Similarly, whenever a person has a setback and slides backward away from that which he desires, he experiences displeasing emotions. This is represented by the frown on the person's face that we see sliding downward.

The purpose of this painting is to illustrate the basic principle that underlies human emotions. Emotional experiences and expressions are always relative to something desirable or undesirable in life. More detailed explanations will soon follow.

Third Word Painting:

In this painting we see two symbolic faces. As in the previous painting with the two mountain-climbing illustrations, one face is smiling and the other frowning.

Interpretation:

The reason for presenting these two faces is to again focus on the essence of the previous painting, namely that emotional feelings are always somewhere on a scale between desirable and undesirable. Examples of such ranges of feeling include:

Happy to Sad

Joyful to Sorrowful

Confident to Fearful

Elation to Anger

Etc.

As we live our lives and pursue our objectives, whatever they may be, we encounter situations that are favorable, unfavorable, or somewhere in between. Favorable situations cause us to experience positive feelings while unfavorable situations cause us to experience the opposite. This painting is obviously a continuation of the ideas presented in the previous one. More detailed explanations will soon follow.

Value Exchanges and Associated Emotions
Another Principle of Human Nature

Fourth Word Painting:

In this painting we are reminded of another that we saw earlier on our tour. We again see those three familiar pairs of faces.

☺ ☺ Win Win

☺ ☹ Win Lose

☹ ☹ Lose Lose

Interpretation:

Throughout our lives we continually exchange value with others. This value that we exchange can be in many different forms, mental and/or physical. Mental value is typically associated with something that is emotionally pleasing. Physical value is often associated with something that has monetary value. Whenever two individuals engage in a value exchange there is a variation of three different outcomes, as represented by the pairs of faces in this painting:

If each person believes that he received something of equal value in exchange for what he contributed, both are pleased and we have a win-win situation.

If one person is satisfied with the value he received but the other decides that he received less value than he contributed, one person is pleased and the other is displeased. We then have a win-lose situation.

If both become dissatisfied with the exchange, we have a lose-lose situation.[3,4]

It is a basic characteristic of human nature that all of us desire to receive comparable value in exchange for what we contribute. This is so ingrained in every person's psyche that it can be referred to as "the law of equal value exchange."

As was explained earlier, many people may be quick to suggest that they freely give their time, talent, and treasure without expecting any compensation in return. This argument can easily be countered with the clarification that these same people DO expect to experience personal emotional satisfaction in exchange for their charitable giving. In other words, through charitable giving they can admire themselves for their personal generosity and feel good about themselves as a result. Such feelings are of immense personal mental value and are powerful motivators.

Systems of Society
Another Principle of Human Nature

Tour Guide's Introduction:

In this section of the gallery, another underlying principle of human nature is presented, one that is often not thought about and one that is more difficult to comprehend and explain. Each and every person (ideally) is a participant in one or more *systems of society*. In this respect, each and every person is a part of a larger whole. This principle was alluded to during a previous gallery tour where it was suggested that each and every person is a cell within a larger body of humanity.

Fifth Word Painting:

In this painting is a basic illustration representing our world economic system. Within this vast system is a network of value exchanges that take place continually on a daily basis all around our planet, many of which are in the form of monetary transactions. As we view this painting in more detail we see that it is a vast system that in turn is comprised of numerous smaller systems. Specific examples include systems for food production, health care, housing, transportation, education, personal guidance, government, building construction, manufacturing, finance, arbitration, entertainment, recreation, and—the list goes on. All of these systems

(Continued on page 156)

(Continued from page 155)

have a single thing in common: All of them serve to fulfill human needs of one type or another.

Each of these systems is made up of individual people engaged in individual career occupations. These people contribute value to their respective systems in the form of their personal time and talent. In return they receive monetary compensation from the respective systems in which they are participating. These people then ex-change this monetary compensation for the goods and services that they need or desire, to live in physical and/or mental comfort.

Interpretation:

What we see in this painting may be viewed as the "real world" or the "material world," at least in some people's perspectives. Each and every person has certain needs and desires. Among them is a desire to live in physical comfort. To fulfill this desire, people usu-ally need money (monetary value) to pay for their basic physical needs—food, clothing, housing, etc. To obtain this monetary value, people normally need some type of career.

As a matter of interest, when enough people have a certain need or desire, and when these same people also have sufficient monetary exchange to offer, somehow and in someway a *system* is created to fill that need or desire. Such is the nature of entrepreneurship and market economics. ☺

Sixth Word Painting:

This painting is a refinement of the previous one. Here we see example illustrations of people engaged in many different career occupations within the world economic system. These include farmers, doctors, nurses, construction workers, truck drivers, pilots, teachers, counselors, nurses, politicians, factory personnel, bankers, lawyers, comedians, athletes, actors, health care providers, and—the list goes on.

Interpretation:

As we view this assortment of career positions that combine to form a world economic system of value exchanges, we notice that a broad diversity of *skills* is required to fill these various positions. As an example, doctors have unique skills that differ from those of bankers, who in turn have skills that differ from those of farmers, and so on. Essentially, what we are seeing in this painting is a diversity of human talent throughout the world economic system.

When people have a choice, they will gravitate to whichever career position they prefer. It is interesting to note that virtually every career position is attractive to certain people. (That is assuming it offers sufficient compensation along with sufficiently comfortable working conditions.)

A question now arises: What is it that attracts a person to a certain career position (aside from issues of monetary compensation and working conditions)? Herein is the basis for another principle of human nature, namely that people enjoy utilizing their natural talents, whatever these talents happen to be. When people are able to utilize them in their employment occupation, they can happily contribute value to others. When they are also fortunate enough to receive equal value in exchange for their employment contributions, they are in a situation that is conducive to life satisfaction and happiness.

Overall, this painting simply illustrates the obvious fact that a diversity of career talents is found throughout the world economic system. Another question now arises: What gives rise to this diversity of talent? Suggested answers are about to be provided in the next painting.

Aptitudes
Another Principle of Human Nature

Tour Guide's Introduction:

The principle of human nature about to be described in this section of our gallery tour is that every person has inner *aptitudes,* and these are *seeds* with the *potential* to grow into career talents. (Whether they ever do or not is another matter.)[5,6]

Seventh Word Painting:

Here again we have a painting that is similar to one encountered earlier on our tour. Since it describes a basic principle of human nature it is presented again here. What we see depicted in this painting is a garden that has already been planted, but from which no plants have yet emerged. Next to this garden we see a sign that reads: *Garden of the Mind. Aptitude Seeds have been planted.*

Interpretation:

As explained earlier on our tour and above, each and every person has certain inner aptitudes and they are the *seeds of talent*. Within a diversity of people these aptitudes can grow, blossom, and mature into a diversity of career skills. This diversity of people with their diversity of skills can interact to comprise a world economic system with a broad diversity of value exchanges.

Also as explained earlier, just because every person is born with aptitudes that have the potential to grow into skills, this does not mean they actually will. The care and guidance of skilled mental gardeners are needed for this to occur.

It is generally recognized that every person needs to somehow participate in the world economic system if he expects to earn the monetary compensation that he will need to live comfortably. Once again, this concept of human aptitudes is easier to comprehend when we realize that they are *seeds* with the potential to grow (under the right conditions) into valuable skills that will enable a person to fill a position in the world economic system and thereby obtain the monetary means to live in comfort.

This concept of human aptitudes is another key facet of human nature. To acquire a basic understanding of another person, it is helpful if one can identify his natural aptitudes and the degree to which they have grown and developed into actual skills.

Something More
Another Principle of Human Nature

Tour Guide's Introduction:

The principle of human nature to be described in this section is that people generally have a natural desire for "something more." Once a certain satisfaction in life is attained, it is often not long before a person will develop a longing for "something more." This longing may be for something material, or for something that is emotional that money alone cannot buy. Many of us have a difficult time identifying exactly what this "something more" actually is. More light is about to be cast upon this subject.

Eighth Word Painting:

In this painting we see two neighborhoods of homes. One is filled with affluent luxurious mansions on expansive picturesque properties. The occupants of these homes apparently have an abundance of monetary wealth. The other neighborhood is filled with more modest homes on smaller properties. While modest in appearance, they still appear to be comfortable dwellings in which to live.

In this same painting we can see the occupants of the homes in both neighborhoods coming and going, as they leave and return from wherever they work, play, go to school, etc. We are thus able to see the expres-

(Continued on page 162)

161

(Continued from page 161)

sions on their faces. As we focus on the people in the affluent neighborhood we see that some of them appear satisfied with their lives, but not all of them. As we focus on the people in the average neighborhood, we see that many of them appear to be just as satisfied with their lives as those in the more affluent neighborhood. These observations cause us to wonder why.

Interpretation:

What this painting is intended to illustrate is a simple fact that is commonly known but still deserves to be mentioned, namely that money alone does not buy happiness. One can earn an abundance of monetary value and still be dissatisfied with life. Or, one can earn a modest amount of income and enjoy considerable life satisfaction.

Every person has a natural desire to live in physical comfort. However, comfortable living conditions can be obtained with a modest amount of monetary income. Beyond that, *something more* is needed to experience life satisfaction. As has been explained in another gallery earlier on this tour, each and every person also needs *mental or emotional value* in addition to monetary value to enjoy life.

Mental value is obtained through mental achievement. This entails personal growth and development:

One area of achievement is the successful conversion of natural aptitudes into marketable skills, as has previously been discussed.

Another area of achievement is the ability to live in accord with one's natural inborn *archetypes*. (This is a new concept for many, and is described in greater detail in the next section.)

And of course, every person needs the personal and social satisfaction of true love and friendship with family and friends. This is a tremendous mental achievement all in it itself. Success in this area encompasses a broad variety of issues including the ability to empathize, which is repeatedly discussed throughout these many gallery tours.

Still another area of achievement is to reach the point where one can recognize inner *inspirations* provided by the Master Artists, and also be willing to follow those inspirations. This is sometimes understood in terms of living in accord with one's conscience.

All of the preceding areas of achievement require that one acquire knowledge and skills, both of which are also forms of mental value.

A very simple summary of the principle of human nature described in this section is that every person needs *something more* than physical value to experience life satisfaction. This *something more* is mental or emotional value in various forms as described herein.

(Note that while the words "conscience" and "consciousness" have similar pronunciations, they are distinctly different from each other. Conscience is one's Inner Inspiration and Guidance. Consciousness is an entity within the human mind that acts as an observer of inner thought and outer activity. Another way to distinguish between these two terms is to consider the following: Through meditation and journaling one can become *conscious of one's conscience*. Admittedly, in certain situations the matter of living in accord with one's conscience can be a major challenge.) ☺

Archetypes
Another Principle of Human Nature

Tour Guide's Introduction:

The principle of human nature to be described in this portion of our gallery tour is one of the more difficult to explain and understand: Within the mind of each and every person are certain *natural inclinations* to play certain dramatic roles on the world stage. These natural inclinations are an outgrowth of inner mental *characteristics* or *predispositions* that are called *archetypes*.[8,9]

Ninth Word Painting:

In this painting we see a large diverse group of people participating in various dramas on the world stage. Each and every person that we see is playing a specific *role* in one or more dramas. There are many different people and many different dramas and hence there are many different roles.

Interpretation:

Upon viewing this painting we may wonder about the reasons why people select their respective roles on the world stage. What draws them to one particular role and not to another? This question can be answered with an introduction to another basic principle of human nature: Each and every person has certain *inner inclinations* to play certain dramatic roles on the world stage. These inner inclinations come naturally to a person, and are an outgrowth of his inner *archetypes*. Or in other words, *archetypes* are inner mental *characteristics* or *predispositions* that can grow and develop into *inclinations* to play certain dramatic roles on the world stage.

It is important to consider that a person can be *inclined* to play a certain role, but still decide not to. Reasons why a person might not follow through with his inclinations include a lack of self-confidence and a lack of opportunity, along with many others.

Examples of various dramatic archetypal roles that are found in many different systems all across the world stage and which people may be *inclined* to pursue are identified with *italics* in the following descriptions:

> Some people are *visionaries*. They strive to express what may be attainable for this world, and the benefits to be obtained.

> Some people are *creators* and *inventors*. They strive to transform visions and ideas into material form.

> Some people are *builders*. They build organizations and systems that provide services to society, sometimes with the aid of new inventions and innovations.

> Some people are *promoters*. They strive to promote and sell ideas, innovations, and/or systems that can somehow benefit others.

> Some people are *leaders*. They strive to lead others in the implementation of ideas and innovations through the construction of systems and organizations.

> Some people are *managers*. They strive to manage systems and organizations that have been created by others.

> Some people are *maintainers*. They strive to maintain what has already been created and provide ongoing support.

Some people are *guides*. They strive to provide help and guidance for those in need.

Some people are *educators*. They strive to provide knowledge to those in need.

Some people are *caregivers*. They strive to help those in need.

Some people are *entertainers*. They strive to provide fun and enjoyment for others.

Some people are *arbitrators*. They strive to resolve conflicts and differences of opinion.

Some people are *artists*. They strive to express love, beauty, and other emotions in artistic form.

Some people are *guardians*. They strive to guard the well being of society and its members.

Some people are *philosophers*. They strive to find order in the midst of chaos, and to make sense out of a bewildering, complex world. ☺

This listing could go on indefinitely.

Once again, deep within the mind of each and every person are mental characteristics or dispositions that are *seeds* with the potential to grow into *inclinations* to play certain *dramatic roles* in various world stage dramas. These mental characteristics or inner dispositions are called *archetypes*.

It is natural to wonder about the origin of these archetypal seeds. Here is a possibility: As most tour participants understand, the physical characteristics of our human bodies are already predetermined at the time of our birth. This predetermination is coded within our genetic DNA. Possibly, our mental archetypal characteristics are also somehow predetermined at the time of our birth.

Maybe these characteristics are also coded within our DNA, or maybe not. Possibly, they are instead formed through early life experiences when one is strongly influenced by the people and events in one's immediate surroundings. The exact origin of these archetypal seeds may forever be debatable.

It is to be noted that each of these archetypal roles can in some way contribute *value* to other individuals and to society as a whole.

As is the case with aptitudes, just because certain archetypal seeds are somehow implanted within the mind of a person, this does not mean that they will actually grow and develop. Some seeds may instead lie dormant throughout a person's life. Some may partially grow but never fully mature. For archetypal seeds to grow, blossom, and reach full maturity, the right growing conditions need to be present. These conditions may include the guidance of competent mentors (mental gardeners) to provide appropriate nourishment that is conducive to healthy mental growth.

Tenth Word Painting:

> In this painting we see a refinement of one that was first seen in the Systems of Society section. We again see the overall world economic system that is composed of many smaller systems, each of which serves a human need. Examples include systems for food production, health care, housing, transportation, education, guidance, government, building construction, manufacturing, finance, arbitration, entertainment, recreation, and—the list goes on.
>
> *(Continued on page 168)*

(Continued from page 167)
In this painting we also see that each of these many systems occupies a certain area on the world stage. In addition, we see that each of these many systems is made up of many individual people, and within each of these systems are many dramas of human interaction. We also see that each and every person is playing a dramatic role within whichever system he participates.

Interpretation:

The various dramatic archetypal roles that have been described and labeled in *italics* during this section of our gallery tour can be enacted within virtually any of the systems of society that are found anywhere on the world stage.

Eleventh Word Painting:

In this painting we see three separate settings on the world stage. One is that of a career environment, similar to those described in the previous painting. Another setting is that of a home and family environment. Still another is that of a social environment. As we focus more closely on these three stage settings we see entirely different dramas being enacted in each. As we focus

(Continued on page 169)

(Continued from page 168)
more closely on the actors, we see that they have the freedom to move from one setting to the next and thereby participate in the distinctly different dramas that are being enacted in each.

Interpretation:

This painting simply illustrates that a person's life can entail simultaneous participation in various different dramas. As an example, a person can play a career role in one drama, a family member role in another drama, and a social role in another. More specifically, a person might be a *manager* in his career role, a *guardian* in his family role, and an *entertainer* in his social role. Typically, the role one *prefers* to play in any particular drama is the result of a *natural inclination* that is a manifestation of an *inner archetype*.

Another issue now arises: For various reasons a person might be compelled or even forced to play a role that does not come naturally to him. Here is a reason why a person may experience emotional discomfort and possibly mental anguish. While this may be easier said than done, the solution to such a person's dilemma may be to discover his natural archetypal role to be played on the world stage and to change his life accordingly.

Twelfth Word Painting:

> This is a simplistic painting in which we see two smiling faces, those of a woman and a man. We may wonder about the underlying reasons for their smiles. Beneath this painting is a title that helps answer our question: *Archetypal Emotional Satisfaction*

Interpretation:

This admittedly simplistic painting is intended to summarize and reinforce a key principle of human nature. Finding and fulfilling dramatic roles on the world stage that are natural outgrowths of a person's inner archetypes are essential for a person to experience emotional satisfaction in life.

Tribute:

In appreciation for his inspiration and influence upon this writer, here is a brief tribute to Carl Jung:

Carl Jung (1875-1961) was a Swiss psychiatrist and psychotherapist. According to the online encyclopedia *wikipedia,* "a *Review of General Psychology Survey,* published in 2002, ranked Jung as the 23rd most cited psychologist of the 20th century." He is credited with originating the concepts of *psychological types*[7] and *archetypes*[8] that are extensively discussed along these

(Continued on page 171)

170

(Continued from page 170)

tours. These concepts have since been greatly expanded upon by numerous writers and psychologists, some of whom are also mentioned and given due credit along this tour. This writer is now expanding upon those concepts with additional ideas of his own. Admittedly, this writer's ideas are theoretical, and are therefore subject to debate. ☺

Tribute:

In appreciation for their inspiration and influence upon this writer, here is a brief tribute to the husband and wife team Tad Guzie and Noreen Monroe Guzie:

Tad Guzie (1934-2001) was a Professor in the Faculty of Education at Calgary University in Calgary, Alberta from 1978 to 2000. He received his PhD from the University of Cambridge in England. Noreen Guzie is an artist and was a frequent workshop director with her husband. Together, they conducted numerous seminars for thousands of people throughout the United States and Canada, during which they described the concepts of human archetypes and how these concepts are central keys to human understanding.

(Continued on page 172)

(Continued from page 171)

They also coauthored a book titled *About Men and Women*[9] which is the best that I have found for explaining these vital concepts in everyday layman's terms.

Also, for anyone who wishes to more clearly understand the differences between archetypes and psychological types, an interesting clarification is provided in the appendix of their book that may be of particular interest to professionals in this field.

In my view this book is an absolute classic that contains a wealth of wisdom from which every person can benefit.

Inner Inspiration
Another Principle of Human Nature

Tour Guide's Commentary:

The principle of human nature to be described in this section is that people can experience a variety of *inner inspirations* through the course of their lives, from childhood on through senior adulthood. Often people choose to live their lives in accord with those inspirations, whatever they may be. In so doing they can find themselves in the midst of challenging dramatic situations on the world stage, sometimes with delightful and sometimes with dire consequences.

Thirteenth Word Painting:

> In this painting we see a person engaged in silent contemplation, with or without a writing instrument. This person is seeking answers to certain questions that he is being confronted with in his life.

Interpretation:

This is also similar to a previous painting along our tour. It illustrates another principle of human nature. Some people engage in silent contemplation during which they solicit the assistance of the Master Artists. They ask questions of these artists. Answers then spontaneously appear within their minds. These answers may arrive while the person is engaged in contemplation or sometime later, sometimes unexpectedly.

173

As we view such a person engaged in silent contemplation, we may understandably question the source of those ideas that somehow spontaneously appear within his mind. This person might presume that those answers originate directly from the Master Artists, and will thereby consider them to be a form of divine revelation. Maybe this person is correct with his assumptions and maybe not. Outside observers might presume that such a person simply has an active imagination, but nothing more. Maybe such outside observers are correct with their presumptions, and maybe not. The answer to this question may forever be debatable.

This painting illustrates another principle of human nature, namely that certain people do engage in silent contemplation and thereby become inspired by certain ideas. Some of them follow through and live their lives in accord with these inner inspirations. Whether these inspirations which account for the activities in their lives are true or false, right or wrong, valid or invalid, is open to question. Also, the source of these inspirations is similarly open to question. The important thing to realize is that right or wrong, various people are motivated through inner inspirations, and these can be a mystery to any observer.

Tour Guide's Commentary:

At this point I will again digress a little. Some people consider themselves to be servants and followers of the *inner word.* Maybe they are and maybe they are not. Other people come to mistakenly believe that they *are* the *inner word.* These same people can be dangerous and lead others astray. Other people, rightly or wrongly, view themselves as philosophers and openly admit that they make mistakes. They caution people to carefully consider any and all ideas, their own as well as others, including *everything* they read and hear, including this manuscript. These self-styled philosophers kindly suggest that people carefully make their own decisions with the aid of their personal inner inspirations, and to be sure that those inspirations are ALWAYS in accord with the Golden Rule. ☺

Fourteenth Word Painting:

> Here we see the same painting that we saw earlier in which there are two neighborhoods. One of the neighborhoods is characterized by affluent monetary wealth. The other is more modest in appearance, but still appears comfortable. Again we see people with smiling faces in each neighborhood, indicating that they are generally pleased with their lives.

Interpretation:

As we view this painting we naturally wonder: "What are all those people smiling about?" Reflecting back over the course of our tour thus far, we have been given certain clues to help explain the reasons why certain people are pleased with their lives, and these include:

Possibly, their natural inner *aptitudes* have grown into career skills. They find life to be pleasing because they are engaged in occupations that utilize their natural talents.

Possibly, their natural inner *archetypes* have grown into archetypal roles in various dramas on the world stage. They find life pleasing because they are enacting natural life roles for which they are uniquely qualified by virtue of their inner archetypes.

Possibly, they are in positions where they are able to receive value from others that is in equal proportion to the value they contribute. As a result they are not experiencing the pain and suffering that comes from unfairness or injustice.

Possibly, while they have the monetary means to live in physical comfort, an overwhelming amount of the value they experience in life is pleasingly *emotional* in nature as explained in this section.

Possibly, they are living in accord with certain *inner inspirations.* Even if their lives appear to be rather austere, *realizing that they are living in accord with their inner inspirations gives their lives a sense of meaning and as a result they experience immense personal emotional satisfaction.*

Emotions
Another Principle of Human Nature

Tour Guide's Introduction:

An obvious principle of human nature is that all of us are emotional beings. This has been repeatedly expressed during various preceding gallery tours. In this particular gallery, with the aid of additional analogies, human emotions are described in greater detail to provide an expanded understanding.[10] Warning! Here comes another of those "twists and turns!"

Fifteenth Word Painting:

Here we see a mural that extends from floor to ceiling along a long wall in this gallery. A vast mountain range is depicted in this mural. Within this range are a variety of different mountains, with varying heights and varying slopes. Some of the slopes are rather steep thereby posing a serious challenge for would-be climbers. Other slopes are more moderate, along which there are clear, well-traveled pathways to the summits. From what we can see, it appears that there are certain challenges associated with any and every mountain that a person might endeavor to climb, with some of those challenges being more difficult than others.

What is of particular interest is the distinctive view from the ascending elevations of various different

(Continued on page 178)

177

(Continued from page 177)

mountains. It is apparent that the higher people climb, the grander will be their view. Realizing that some mountains are taller than others, one can also see that the views from intermediate points on taller mountains are grander than the summit views of other mountains that are not as tall.

Inscribed in this mural, at the base of this vast array of mountains, is a sign that reads *"Value Vision Range"*.

Interpretation:

While this mural painting is decidedly different in appearance, its interpretation follows somewhat logically from those of previous paintings.

As explained before, every person has an inner treasure trove of *value visions*. To somehow someday experience such a vision is analogous to the challenges one would face when endeavoring to climb a mountain. Some visions are more difficult to achieve than others, just as some mountains are more difficult to climb than others. Similarly, some visions are more easily attained just as some mountains are easier to climb. People who pursue grand visions as might only be experienced in certain career positions are faced with difficult challenges, just as the climbers of the tallest mountains are. At the same time, the higher they manage to climb, the grander will be their view, whether or not they ever reach the summit.

Sixteenth Word Painting:

This is another mural showing the same *Value Vision Range* of mountains that we saw in the previous mural. Something has been added, namely a sign at the foot of each individual mountain revealing its name. As we read each name we notice it is that of a career position, and we also notice there is a mountain named after virtually every *career position* to which a person might aspire.

As we study this mural in more detail, we notice that in addition to mountains with career position names other mountains are named after *desirable life situations*. These include such names as *Family Appreciation, Social Harmony, Romantic Love, Recreational Stimulation, Adventurous Travel, Peace and Harmony, Mental Well-Being, Charitable Satisfaction, Life Understanding, World Peace,* and a host of others.

As we study this mural in even more detail, we also notice that some of the mountains have *combination names.* Typically these comprise a combination of a career position and several desirable life situations.

Interpretation:

This mural essentially provides an expanded clarification of the explanation provided for the previous mural. The vision of life that one desires can be experienced at the summit of a certain *value vision* mountain. However, before that vision can be experienced,

179

one must acquire the skills and resources needed to climb that mountain. Once those skills and resources are acquired, one must have the persistence to follow through with the climb. In addition, one must have the willingness to deal with obstacles and problems as they are encountered along this upward climb.

Once again, it is to be noted that many mountains have *combination names.* This is because a person will typically choose a mountain that offers multiple views at its summit. These multiple views encompass those of a certain career position that a person desires, along with other desirable life situations that he wishes to experience, particularly in his private life.

What is of particular interest to us in regard to virtually every person we encounter throughout our lives are both the specific mountain he has chosen to climb and the views he expects to experience at its summit. What is also of interest are the challenges that he faces along his upward climb and how he responds to those challenges. For additional insights, we proceed with this gallery tour.

Seventeenth Word Painting:

Here is another mural that again depicts the *Value Vision Range* of mountains. Once again, the same mountains with the same identification signs are shown. However, in this painting we see another addition, namely multitudes of people many of whom are at various stages in their ascent on many (but not all) of the mountains. Some have reached the summits, particular-

(Continued on page 181)

(Continued from page 180)

ly those mountains with lower elevations. Others are still near the base of various mountains, having just begun their climbs. Some are still contemplating which mountains to climb and which preparations need to be made. Still others have surveyed the vast selection of mountains and decided that it is not worth their time or effort to climb any of them. Most are at various intermediate points somewhere along their upward ascents.

As we more closely examine the various climbers in this mural we see that they are experiencing various *personal emotions*, all of which are a direct result of the situations they are encountering along their upward ascents. Below this painting we see a series of brief explanations that describe these climbers' varied emotional states. In each explanation the name of the emotion being described is identified in *italics*. These explanations with *italicized* names read as follows:

> Some of the climbers who are at the top are expressing *jubilation*. Some are jubilant for having met the associated challenges and for their success in making the climb. Others are jubilant because they are enjoying the summit view. Others are jubilant for both reasons.

> For some of the climbers who have attained their summit views the emotion of *jubilation* (which is usually temporary) has gradually worn off. Still

(Continued on page 182)

(Continued from page 181)

they remain *pleased* with their achievements and associated summit views. These individuals are exhibiting the emotions of *satisfaction* and *contentment* with what they have accomplished.

Some of the climbers who are at the summits of certain mountains are expressing *disappointment.* For them the view is not as grand as they thought it would be, or not even at all what they thought it would be.

Some of the climbers who are at the top are expressing *regret* for having invested the time, energy, and expense to climb this mountain that ultimately provided such a *disappointing* view.

Some of the climbers who are still near the bottom are expressing the emotion of *frustration.* They are *frustrated* because they are unable to advance, even though they would really like to. Some are frustrated because they are ill prepared. Some are frustrated because they are lacking in mountain climbing experience and skills. Similarly, some are frustrated because they are lacking in the necessary knowledge of how to make the climb. Some are frustrated for a variety of other reasons that are preventing their ascent. Still, even though they are frustrated, they can still have *hope* that solutions to their problems can somehow be found.

(Continued on page 183)

(Continued from page 182)

As with those climbers near the bottom, some of the climbers at intermediate points are also expressing *frustration*. This is because they have encountered obstacles and problems. For what could be any number of reasons their upward progress has been halted and they feel *frustrated* as a result. Still they may have the belief that their problems can be solved and that their obstacles can be overcome. They may therefore still have *hope* that sooner or later their upward ascent can continue.

Some climbers or would-be climbers encounter obstacles that they believe cannot be overcome. They do not believe that their problems can be solved and therefore have no hope for any solution. These individuals experience the emotion of *discouragement* and possibly suffer greatly.

Some of the climbers at intermediate locations are experiencing the emotion of *fear*. They are fearful of a situation that could harm them. They are *fearful* of potential injury—possibly one that is fatal. Maybe their fears are realistic and therefore caution is advised. Maybe their fears are unrealistic, and an effort to overcome them is advised. Either way, those climbers who sense potential injury are experiencing the emotion of *fear*.

(Continued on page 184)

(Continued from page 183)

Some of the climbers at intermediate locations are expressing *joy*. Possibly they have encountered an obstacle and through certain efforts have succeeded in overcoming it. Possibly, they have encountered another desirable situation, either through chance or through careful planning and effort. As a result of something positive that has occurred, they feel *joyful*.

Some of the climbers are expressing *anger*. They have encountered an obstacle on their upward climb. They can *see* what the obstacle is. It may be a thing or it may be a person. If there is nothing they can do to remove or overcome this obstacle, they will experience the emotion of *anger*. This anger is directed at the person or thing that has obstructed their advancement up the mountain.

A few climbers have reached a certain point on their upward climb after which they are blocked from advancing further by other individuals. If those others who are blocking the way have somehow attained an unfair advantage through theft or dishonesty, these climbers who are being blocked will experience the emotion of *resentment* toward those who have unfairly halted their advancement.

While some climbers experience difficulty with their climbs, they simultaneously observe others

(Continued on page 185)

(Continued from page 184)

ascending with ease. While these climbers do not begrudge the success of others, at the same time they *wish* they could be similarly successful. In so doing they experience the emotion of *envy*. Again, they do not *resent* others success, they simply wish they could be similarly successful. One reason why they do not begrudge others of their success may be because they can see that those others have achieved their success fairly and squarely. As a result they *admire* others for the success they have achieved. *Admiration* is also a form of emotion.

Here is a variation on the emotion of *envy* and it is *jealously*. When a climber aspires to a certain position at the summit, it might be denied because another person succeeds in obtaining that position instead. Particularly if there is only enough space for one person in that summit position, one might then experience the emotion of *jealousy* toward that person for obtaining something that one wanted for himself. This feeling could be intensified with feelings of *resentment* if the successful person obtained that position unfairly through dishonesty.

Some climbers sincerely hope to make their ascent and experience the summit view along with a certain companion. A few of these climbers have had their companions abandon them for the company of another person. Those climbers can experience the

(Continued on page 186)

(Continued from page 185)
emotion of *jealousy* toward the person for whom their desired companion has abandoned them.

Some of the climbers are expressing *sorrow*. They have experienced a form of loss and feel *sorrowful* as a result. Maybe they have experienced an injury. Maybe they have had a monetary loss. Maybe they have lost a family member. Maybe they have lost a friendship. Having experienced a personal setback or loss in one form or another, they experience the emotion of *sorrow*.

Some individuals lose interest in pursuing their value visions. Maybe they don't know how to advance or are not willing to invest the necessary time and energy. As a result they are not experiencing any of the adventure associated with climbing a mountain to experience a value vision. Due to this lack of adventure in their life they experience the emotion of *boredom* as a result.

Some climbers have encountered problems that are delaying their ascent. At the same time they are not giving up. They are busy searching for solutions to their problems, solutions that will enable them to continue with their upward ascent. They experience feelings of *hope* that such solutions can be found. Some feel very sure that they will find appropriate solutions and thus experience the emotions of *optimism* and *confidence*.

(Continued on page 187)

(Continued from page 186)

Some climbers discover other climbers who are able to assist them with their upward climb. Some of these climbers sincerely wish to help others advance as much as they do themselves. Some of these climbers form teams in which they mutually help each other. These climbers experience emotional feelings of *friendship* with each other.

Here and there two climbers discover and get to know each other to an extent where they form a bond, become a team of two, and advance together. These two climbers experience *love* for each other and are to be *admired*.

Interpretation:

Most people attempt to climb certain mountains for the purpose of experiencing certain value visions at the summits of those mountains. Along their climbs upward, every person encounters a series of emotional experiences for any number of reasons. When advancements are made, their emotions include pleasant feelings of joy, happiness, and jubilation. When setbacks occur, their emotions may include such unpleasant feelings as fear, anger, sadness, and sorrow. Overall, human emotions span a broad spectrum of feelings from desirable to undesirable, with many subtle variations in between.

As people pursue their value visions they enact their roles on the world stage and their lives become a series of dramatic, emotional experiences. Each and every person is inherently emotional—this is a basic part of our fundamental human nature.

187

Tribute:

In appreciation for his inspiration and influence upon this writer, here is a brief tribute to Kenneth Bullmer:

Kenneth Bullmer (1923-1995) was a professor in the Department of Counseling and Personnel at Western Michigan University. The *Kenneth Bullmer Scholarship for Doctoral Studies in Counseling Psychology* is now annually issued there in his honor.

His book titled *The Art of Empathy—A Manual for Improving Accuracy of Interpersonal Perception*[10] neatly explains primary human emotions in clear objective form. It has been a valuable resource for this writer during his quest for human understanding. Unfortunately, its copyright is in the year 1975, and at the time of this composition (year 2017) is out of print. A few pre-read copies are still available from online booksellers. In my view, this book definitely deserves to someday be reprinted.

Psychological Types
Another Principle of Human Nature

Tour Guide's Introduction:

Here is another interesting principle of human nature, namely that virtually every person is of a certain psychological type.[7,11,12,13] This concept has now been widely accepted thanks to the contributions of various esteemed psychologists, some of whom will be mentioned along this tour. In all there are sixteen psychological types. As you are about to see, our mental theater model will serve as a convenient means for explaining the basics of each.

Eighteenth Word Painting:

In this painting we again see that now familiar human mentality in the form of a mental theater. Within this theater we again see our good friend Consciousness. We also see those two screens upon which Consciousness focuses his attention. One of them is the inner thought world screen. The other is the outer world screen with its view of the world stage through the five senses, especially those of sight and sound.

In this same painting we also see the projector room, which is occupied by another of our friends, namely Sub-consciousness. It is he who determines which thoughts are to appear on the inner thought world screen. He operates beneath the level of Consciousness's awareness. As a result, Consciousness often

(Continued on page 190)

(Continued from page 189)
does not know what Sub-consciousness is contemplating or which thoughts will appear next. The reason is that Sub-consciousness often operates independently and is often NOT under the control of Consciousness.

Interpretation:

Once again, this model has been developed in some detail in certain preceding galleries. The reason it is presented again here is to provide a frame of reference. With the use of this model, the concepts of psychological type are more easily explained.

Nineteenth Word Painting: (E-I Preference)[11,12,13]

In this painting the mental theaters of two individuals are shown. We see both of them simultaneously, and only one difference between the two is depicted. One person's consciousness is becoming energized while focusing on the outer world screen. The other person's consciousness is becoming energized while focusing on his inner thought world screen. From what we can see in this painting, both are healthy, active, vibrant individuals. Their only difference is in which screen those two individuals *prefer* to focus their attention to become energized and mentally refreshed.

Interpretation:

In terms of Psychological Type, this is the basic difference between Extraversion and Introversion. An emphasis is to be placed upon the word *preference*. There may be times when extraverts enjoy focusing on their inner thought world screens, and similarly there may be times when introverts enjoy focusing on the outer world stage. Still, when free to choose, and especially when in need of some mental rejuvenation, extraverts are likely to seek interaction with people in the outer world, while introverts are likely to seek stimulation on their inner mental screen of thoughts and ideas.

Once again, the word *preference* is to be emphasized. Extraverts can develop intellectual reasoning skills, and introverts can develop social interaction skills. Again, when they are in need of some revitalization, the difference can usually be noted: Extraverts are likely to opt for social interaction, possibly with people in their immediate vicinity. Introverts are likely to opt for inner contemplation, possibly with the aid of reading material. There will always be exceptions, but in general these will be their attention preferences when they have a need to be mentally refreshed.

In terms of Psychological Type, this concept is viewed as the E-I preference, E for Extraversion and I for Introversion. It is natural and entirely acceptable to be one or the other.

Twentieth Word Painting: (S-N Preference)[11,12,13]

This painting is similar to the previous one in that the mental theaters of two individuals are shown. In the previous painting we observed two alternate methods of rejuvenation, namely two alternate techniques whereby people become mentally energized and refreshed. In this present painting we instead see two alternate techniques for gathering information to be used for decision -making.

As we browse the outer world screen and inner thought screen in one of these two mental theaters, we see that Consciousness has a preference for actual, obvious, provable information from the physical world, past and present, with which to base his decisions. "Seeing is believing" is the motto of this person, that is "seeing" what has happened and is happening on the world stage.

In contrast, as we browse the outer world screen and inner thought screen in the other mental theater, we see that Consciousness is only partially focused on actual, provable information from the physical world. In this mental theater, we see that Sub-consciousness is busy creating and projecting novel ideas onto the inner thought screen that in many cases are new, different, and have yet to be proven. We also see that Consciousness in this theater is fascinated by those projected ideas from Sub-consciousness, and loves to give them a try even if they are new, unproven, and in some cases appear ridiculous to others.

Interpretation:

In terms of Psychological Type, what we see in this painting with its two mental theaters is the basic difference between Sensing and Intuition. This is referred to as the S-N preference. "S" for sensing, and "N" is for intuition. (Notice that the letter "I" has already been taken to represent "introversion," so the letter "N" is instead utilized to represent "intuition.")

Both types are equally acceptable. Of the two, the sensing type is easier to understand and explain. Since the intuitive type is more mysterious and difficult to comprehend, a more lengthy explanation is needed.

When a sensing person is seeking information with which to make decisions, he is primarily interested in observable facts and events that are taking place on the world stage, or have taken place there. An advantage with this approach is that one can usually provide a rational explanation for the basis of one's decision. One can usually explain how information was obtained because it is easily observable for all to see on the outer world stage, or in records of events that have already occurred there. A disadvantage is that key insights are not always apparent on the outer world stage, especially when there is a need for all-new innovative ideas.

When an intuitive person is seeking information with which to make decisions, he likewise searches the outer world stage for information. However, he also has a keen interest in any ideas that his subconscious mind projects forward upon his inner thought screen. An intuitive person is likely to have discovered that when novel ideas somehow become illuminated upon his inner thought screen, these ideas can sometimes prove to be amazingly correct even if they first appear illogical and maybe even preposterous to most other people. An advantage with this approach is that such information can sometimes pave the way towards brilliant solutions. A disadvantage is that ideas derived in this way can sometimes be difficult to rationally explain without actually trying them. Another disadvantage is that such mysteriously derived ideas can sometimes be proven wrong, much to the embarrassment of the person involved because to logical thinking people those ideas appeared to be completely ridiculous right from the start, and were never worth considering.

It may be suggested that there is less risk for the sensing types because they can usually provide logical explanations for how their information was acquired, and how it was used as a basis for their decisions. As a result, they are subject to less criticism. There is more risk for the intuitive types because it can be difficult for them to explain how they acquired certain ideas, thus they can be subject to more criticism. However, along with more risk is the potential for more reward when intuitively acquired ideas sometimes prove to be surprisingly correct. Throughout history there are examples of intuitive insights that were first strongly criticized, but which ultimately led to impressive results. The invention of the airplane by the Wright brothers is a classic example.

Twenty-First Word Painting: (T-F Preference)[11,12,13]

In this painting we again see the mental theaters of two different individuals. Based upon what we see, we are unable to determine if they are extraverted or introverted individuals. Similarly we are unable to determine how they gather their information for decision-making, whether they are sensing or intuitive individuals. The only difference between these two mental theaters that we can see is the method of mental reasoning that Consciousness utilizes for making his decisions:

Consciousness in one of the theaters tends to make decisions based upon what "looks" like a logical, rational and efficient course of action.

Consciousness in the other theater tends to make decisions based upon what "feels" like a harmonious course of action, one that is harmonious with those who will be affected by the decisions.

Interpretation:

Those who prefer to make decisions based upon what appears to be a logical, rational and efficient course of action have what is known as the "T" preference, "T" for "thinking". Sometimes a person with this preference will tend to make decisions without realizing how others may be affected by his decisions.

Those who prefer to make decisions based upon what "feels" like a harmonious, more conflict free course of action have what is known

195

as the "F" preference, "F" for "feeling". It is important to clarify that this is also a thinking process, only of a different kind that is more emotionally based. Sometimes a person with this preference will tend to make decisions that are intended to *please* as many people as possible without giving due consideration to the practicality of those decisions.

What "looks" right to a person with the "T" preference might not "feel" right to a person with the "F" preference, possibly because certain people may be offended by the proposed course of action. Similarly, what "feels" right to a person with the "F" preference might not "look" right to a person with the "T" preference, possible because the proposed course of action appears impractical to implement.

One can argue that for a course of action to be practical, it must also have the approval of others. To some extent this is true. Still, a person with the "T" preference is likely to place a higher priority on practicality and efficiency, and only enough devotion to harmony as is required to "get the job done as soon as possible." Similarly, a person with the "F" preference is likely to place a higher priority on maintaining harmonious relationships, and only enough devotion to practicality as is required to finally "get the job done sooner or later."

What is often needed is a *blend* of the two thinking processes. Hence people with "T" preferences are encouraged to become more sensitive to other people's feelings. Similarly, people with "F" preferences are encouraged to become more aware of what is practical and realistic.

It is natural for people to prefer one mode of reasoning or the other. Both are valid. Both have advantages in some situations and disadvantages in others. Once again, it is helpful to understand and to appreciate the positive aspects of both.

Twenty-Second Word Painting: (J-P Preference)[11,12,13]

In this painting we again see the mental theaters of two different individuals. This is similar to the previous painting in that we are unable to determine if these are extraverted or introverted individuals. Similarly, we are unable to determine *how* they gather information for decision-making, whether they are sensing or intuitive individuals. In addition, we are unable to determine the methods they use to make decisions, whether they have "thinking" or "feeling" preferences.

We are able to see the Inner Thought Screen in each of these two theaters, and as a matter of particular interest we can see two distinct *zones of thought* on each screen. We can also see that the Consciousness in one of these theaters has a *preference* for one of these zones, while the Consciousness in the other theater has a *preference* for the other. These two zones are titled: *Before a Decision is Made,* and *After a Decision is Made.*

More specifically, the Consciousness in the first theater is more at ease *before a* decision is made. He might not be at ease with the issue to be decided upon, but he is comfortable with the realization that there is still time to gather more information before making an actual decision.

(Continued on page 198)

(Continued from page 197)
In direct contrast, the Consciousness in the second theater is more at ease *after a* decision has been made. He
might not be at ease with the course of action that has
been decided upon, but he is comfortable with the realization that an actual decision has been made and can
now be implemented.

Interpretation:

In terms of Psychological Type this is the basic difference between
the Judging and Perceiving Types. This difference is referred to as
the J-P preference, obviously "J" for judging and "P" for perceiving.

A "P" person is more at ease *before* a decision is made, while engaged in the *perceiving* process during which he can continue to
gather additional information. Once a decision has been reached,
he may feel a little ill at ease wondering if the right decision has
been made. As a result he may continue to gather additional information and be receptive to revising earlier decisions based upon
newly discovered data.

A "J" person is more at ease *after* a decision has been made, *after*
the *judging* (decision making process) is finished. Once made, he
prefers to enact that decision and move onward, feeling comfortable
that enough information was gathered to justify that decision. He is
then reluctant to revise that decision and change his earlier decided
course of action, even if newly discovered information is presented.

It is to be clarified that both the "P" and "J" individuals may be un-
comfortable with the issue to be decided upon. Their primary dif-

ference is that the "P" person is more comfortable when the decision options are still open, while the "J" person is more comfortable after actual decisions have been made and are in the process of implementation.

An advantage associated with the Perceiving preference is that by taking enough time to gather as much information as possible, a foundation is laid for responsible decision-making. Certain people with this preference thereby gain a reputation for being responsible decision makers.

A disadvantage associated with the Perceiving preference is that certain people can delay decisions indefinitely, and even be afraid to make decisions for fear of mistakes. As a result, needed courses of action can be delayed due to lack of confidence. In addition, after a decision has been made there may be a tendency to revise it later. For those who have a tendency to "change their minds," it can be difficult to trust them. One may never know if they will actually follow-through and implement their decisions, or if they will change their minds later. Some of these people are sometimes viewed as being "inconclusive" and "wishy-washy." ☺

An advantage associated with the Judging preference is that these people tend to stick with their decisions. People who do what they say they will do and thereby honor their commitments are usually revered. We value those who do, and criticize those who do not. People with this preference are often admired for their reliability.

A disadvantage associated with the Judging preference is that certain people can be in too much of a hurry to make a decision. With a strong desire to make a decision some individuals may jump to conclusions, without having carefully considered enough information to justify their decision. Once they are "resting assured" that a decision has been made, it can be difficult to convince such individuals to reconsider their decisions on the basis of new information. Even when convincing facts are presented that were not available earlier, such individuals may be reluctant to change their minds. Some of these people are sometimes viewed as being "obstinate" and "set in their ways." ☺

Here again, it is natural for some people to have a "P" preference and for others to have a "J" preference. There are advantages and disadvantages with each. Depending upon the situation, one or the other preference may be advantageous.

Tour Guide's Commentary:

In case you would like some clarification regarding how there can be sixteen different basic psychological types using this methodology, consider the following:

There are four pairs of preferences: E-I, S-N, T-F and J-P

With these four pairs of preferences, there are sixteen combinations:

ESTJ, ISTJ, ESFJ, ISFJ

ESTP, ISTP, ESFP, ISFP

ENTJ, INTJ, ENFJ, INFJ

ENTP, INTP. ENFP, INFP

Please realize that the information in this section on Psychological Types is merely a series of basic explanations. This subject as a whole is much broader. You are strongly encouraged to review the following tributes and to read the recommended texts. In so doing you will be pleased to discover a whole new world of human understanding that is rich with practical applications for everyday living.

Tribute:

In appreciation for their inspiration and influence upon this writer, here is a brief tribute to Katherine Cook Briggs (1875-1968) and her daughter Isabel Briggs Myers (1897-1980):

Through extensive research with hundreds and perhaps thousands of people whom they interviewed and tested, this mother and daughter team made enormous advancements in the understanding of psychological types, having been inspired by the earlier ideas of Carl Jung. The results of their work are neatly explained in the book *Gifts Differing*[11] by Isabel Briggs Myers.

A popular psychology test for determining psychological types with which many are familiar is titled the *Myers-Briggs Type Indicator (MBTI)*. Millions have now taken this same test or a similar one. Just about everybody who studies these concepts is amazed by the insights they provide for understanding themselves and others.

Additional information regarding this mother-daughter team and their life's work can be found at the website www.myersbriggs.org .

Tribute:

In appreciation for their inspiration and influence upon this writer, here is a brief tribute to David Kiersey and Marilyn Bates.

★★★

David Keirsey (1921-2013) and Marilyn Bates were trainers of therapists and diagnosticians of dysfunctional behavior at California State University (Fullerton Campus). Together they wrote the book *Please Understand Me*,[12] which is an enhancement of many ideas proposed by Isabel Briggs Myers in her book *Gifts Differing*.[11] Later, David Keirsey wrote a sequel titled *Please Understand Me II*.[13] He was a psychologist and professor emeritus at California State. Little additional information is available about Marilyn Bates except that she was a coauthor of the first book.

Both of these *Please Understand Me* books provide indepth descriptions of the sixteen different psychological types. Many people who study them remark that they have discovered their own personality accurately described in the form of a certain psychological type, one of the sixteen. Similarly, they discover accurate descriptions of many people they know, also in the form of a specific psychological type. Using the book *Gifts Differing* as a foundation, these two *Please Understand Me* books are likewise intriguing and provide a broadened understanding of this fascinating field. Virtually any person can find them to be both enjoyable and educational.

★★★

Belief Systems
Another Principle of Human Nature

Tour Guide's Introduction:

Another basic principle of human nature is that within each and every human mind is a network of beliefs that have been formed through a series of life experiences from infancy onward through childhood, adolescence, and adulthood. These beliefs combine to form a system that is at the heart of a person's decision-making processes and guides him all through life.[1]

Twenty-Third Word Painting:

In this painting we see a single mental theater as described previously. Again we see Consciousness observing both an outer world screen and an inner thought screen. We also see Sub-consciousness in the projector room busily projecting thoughts onto the thought screen. From what we can see in this painting it is not clear what this person's Psychological Type may be. However, we see that something new has been added in this painting that was not observed before. In the projector room we see a file cabinet of recordings that is labeled "Beliefs." From this file cabinet, Sub-consciousness is able to choose various "belief recordings" and project them onto the inner thought screen whenever he chooses to do so, depending upon whatever situation Consciousness may be encountering on the outer world stage at any given time.

Interpretation:

Whenever a person makes a decision in regard to a certain situation, not only does he seek information on the outer world stage as a basis for his decision, he also factors in his preconceived beliefs relative to that situation. These beliefs are flashed onto his internal thought screen by his subconscious mind.

Examples of basic beliefs that guide a person's decision-making through the course of his life can be described in the form of questions as follows:

What does he believe to be desirable in life?

What does he value?

In terms of family, friends, education, career, and voluntary endeavors, what does he believe to be important?

What does he believe is worth pursuing in life?

What does he believe is within his ability to accomplish?

What does he believe are his personal talents and abilities?

What does he believe to be the best course of action for achieving that which he desires?

What does he believe to be the necessary steps that will lead him to that which he desires?

What does he believe to be the right pathway for him to follow in life?

What does he believe about himself?

What does he believe are his positive attributes?

What does he believe are his negative attributes?

What does he believe about others?

What does he believe are their positive attributes?

What does he believe are their negative attributes?

What does he believe about the world in general?

What does he believe is good about the world?

What does he believe is bad about the world?

This listing of example beliefs is not intended to be all-inclusive; it could go on indefinitely. Instead, the intent in this section is to describe the underlying concept of another fundamental principle of human nature: As stated in the introduction to this section, every person has an internal structure of beliefs that form the basis for the decisions he makes through the course of his life. As a result, a person's many actions and activities on the world stage are a reflection of his internal belief structure.

Tribute:

In appreciation for his inspiration and influence upon this writer, here is a brief tribute to Milton Rokeach:

★★★
★   ★
★   Milton Rokeach (1918-1988) was a social psychologist   ★
★   and professor who taught at Michigan State University,   ★
★   the University of Western Ontario, Washington State   ★
★   University, and the University of Southern California.   ★
★   His books include *Beliefs, Attitudes, and Values*[1] and   ★
★   *The Nature of Human Values.*[2]   ★
★   ★
★   With an objective professional writing style he explains   ★
★   how a person's individual beliefs, attitudes, and values   ★
★   ★
★   *(Continued on page 206)*   ★
★★

★★
(Continued from page 205)

govern his decision making through the entire course of his life. According to the online encyclopedia *Wikipedia*, a *Review of General Psychology* survey, published in 2002, ranked him as the 85th most cited psychologist of the 20th century.
★★

Belief Formation
Another Principle of Human Nature

Tour Guide's Introduction:

Realizing that people's beliefs can be broadly diverse and often in disagreement with others, it is natural to wonder why there is such disagreement. The answer lies in understanding how a person's beliefs are formed. An overly simplistic summary explanation is that a person's beliefs are formed by and through the many positive and negative people and experiences that he encounters along his pathway through life. Here, we are entering the realms of Developmental Psychology, which is a study of the many influences that shape a person's mentality through the course of his life from childhood on through adolescence and adulthood.[14,15] What is especially fascinating is the study of mental formation during childhood and what a permanent effect this can have on a person throughout the remainder of his life.[16,17] A more thorough explanation could entail writing another complete book. For anyone who has the interest, such books have already been written, examples of which are provided in the following three tributes:

Tribute:

In appreciation for his inspiration and influence upon this writer, here is a brief tribute to Stanley Greenspan:

★★

Stanley Greenspan (1941-2010) was Clinical Professor of Psychiatry and Pediatrics at George Washington University Medical School and a practicing child psychiatrist. As an experienced pediatrician, he coauthored many books, mostly focusing upon issues of early childhood development. These included *Growth of the Mind and the Endangered Origins of Intelligence*[16] written with Beryl Lieff Benderly, and *Building Healthy Minds: The Six Experiences that Create Intelligence and Emotional Growth in Babies and Young Children*[17] written with Nancy Breslau Lewis. Both of these books can be appealing to both laymen and professionals alike.

Dr. Greenspan repeatedly emphasizes the extreme importance of early childhood nurturing and care that is so often misunderstood and neglected, thereby causing dire consequences for a child's personality development. Realizing that many parents on all levels of society delegate a substantial portion of their children's training to outside daycare centers where due attention may be lacking, he sounds an alarm for every parent in every walk of life. Any parent who sincerely wishes to get their children off to a mentally healthy start in life will benefit immensely from the insights that he shares.

(Continued on page 208)

★★

(Continued from page 207)

As a matter of interest, one can conclude that there is much to be said for "the good old days" when mothers did not need to enter the workplace and could thereby spend more time with their children. Also, there is much to be said for those family situations in which retired grandparents are available to assist with chil-drearing. The stark realities of today's society are such that it is commonly necessary for both parents to serve as breadwinners and spend considerable time away from home, thereby diminishing the amount of attention they can personally devote to their children. Child mentalities can thus develop with certain deficiencies and anxieties that might otherwise have been avoided. This of course is a highly controversial subject that can be a source for considerable debate. For further and more specific clarifications on what is needed, it is best to refer directly to Dr. Greenspan's books.

Tribute:

In appreciation for his inspiration and influence upon this writer, here is a brief tribute to Elton B. McNeil:

★★★

Elton B. McNeil (1924-1974) was Professor of Psychology at the University of Michigan. He was also President of the Michigan Psychological Association and the Michigan Association of School Psychologists. Among various psychology books that he wrote and co-wrote is a college textbook titled *Human Socialization*.[14] This book neatly describes how a person develops in accord with the social influences of surrounding environments to ultimately form his individual traits, character, goals, personality, and life role preferences. For anyone interested in cause and effect relationships in personal growth and development, this book provides clear insights.

★★★

Tribute:

In appreciation for their inspiration and influence upon this writer, here is a brief tribute to the husband and wife team George and Meriem Fair Kaluger:

★★

George Kaluger (1921-2007) was a Professor at Shippensburg University in Shippensburg, Pennsylvania, and Meriem Fair Kaluger (1921-2006) was a psychologist and educational consultant there. Amongst many professional accomplishments, they wrote a fascinating college textbook together on developmental psychology titled *Human Development – The Span of Life.*[15] Through the course of some 600 pages they describe the personal growth and development process through every phase of life from infancy on through childhood, adolescence, adulthood, and old age. In layman's terms, this book provides an interesting explanation of why and how people become as they are. In many ways this book is a continuation and enhancement of Elton B. McNeil's book *Human Socialization,* which they cite as a reference.

★★

Levels of Consciousness
Another Principle of Human Nature

Tour Guide's Introduction:

Another principle of human nature is that there are *levels of consciousness* from which the various dramas on the world stage can be viewed.[18,19,20,21] Simplistic dramas are easily seen and understood at lower levels. More complex dramas can only be comprehended when viewed from higher levels. A general explanation of this concept is provided in this gallery. As with belief formation, a more thorough explanation could entail writing another book. Once again, for anyone who has the interest such books have also already been written, examples of which are provided in a tribute to follow.

Twenty-Fourth Word Painting:

> Here we see a painting that is similar to one presented during an earlier gallery tour. Again we see a mental theater with two screens, an outer world screen and an inner thought screen. What is unique about this painting is that within the audience section of this theater are two seats for observers. One is occupied by the person's Consciousness. The other seat is unoccupied.

Interpretation:

As explained previously, the ultimate form of Empathy would be for one's Consciousness to enter the mental theater of another person and occupy that empty seat, from which one could observe both screens. While this idea helps to explain the concept of empathy, realistically it is not possible for one person's consciousness to enter the mental theater of another. With this realization we proceed to view and consider the next painting.

Twenty-Fifth Word Painting:

> This is another painting that is similar to one we observed during an earlier gallery tour. This is the painting in which we see Consciousness and Sub-consciousness busily creating audio-visual presentations of people's life dramas for private viewing within their mental theatre.

Interpretation:

As Consciousness and Sub-consciousness create these audio-visual presentations they are endeavoring to *empathize* with people, namely to see and understand the lives of others from the perspective of those others. The degree to which one can empathize with other individuals is an indication of one's level of consciousness. **As one learns to empathize with more and more people and as one learns to understand increasingly complex facets of people's lives, one's level of consciousness rises accordingly.** To help explain this in more detail, consider the many different aspects of life:

> Consider the bodies of humanity and the cells within these bodies, each of which is an actual human being.

Consider the many systems within these bodies, examples of which include: family, social, recreational, educational, philosophical, economic, governmental, etc. All of these systems have something in common in that they are designed to provide some combination of mental and emotional value to the people they serve.

Consider the many different positions that people occupy within these systems.

Consider the various levels of responsibility within these systems.

Consider the many different types of value exchanges that take place between individuals within these systems.

Consider the many different individuals aspiring to various positions within these systems.

Consider the many different motivations and goal plans that people have to advance within these systems and become situated in desirable positions. Consider the challenges they face, and the obstacles they encounter.

Consider the many different emotional experiences that people encounter across the broad spectrum of human emotions, from extreme pleasure to extreme pain.

The more one is able to empathize with individuals and the many complexities they face in all aspects of their lives in our broad diversity of world situations, the higher will be one's level of consciousness. Another way of saying this is that the higher one's level of consciousness happens to be, the greater will be one's understanding of the many *varied and diverse dramas* of human life taking place all around this planet amongst all groups of people and at all levels of society.

As a matter of interest, along with the attainment of higher levels of consciousness and increased human understanding is an increasing desire to make one's life a *true work of art*. This is the subject of Part 4 of these gallery tours.

Again, additional explanations of levels of consciousness and how they are attained are available in other texts by other authors. A tribute to one of them now follows.

Tribute:
In appreciation for his inspiration and influence upon this writer, here is a brief tribute to Brian P. Hall:

★★★

Brian P. Hall (1935-2013) was the founder and President of Values Technology, www.valuestech.com. His primary life work was in values research.

According to the website, working with an international team in the 1970's, he posited 125 values that underpin human behavior. At the University of Santa Clara, he developed a measurement instrument, validated by the American Psychological Association, for those 125 values, including applications for individual and group values measurement.

He was an Episcopal Priest and his various career positions included Professor of Pastoral Counseling and Counseling Psychology at Santa Clara University in California, and Adjunct Professor of St. Mary's College of California graduate programs in leadership.

(Continued on page 215)

★★★

★★

(Continued from page 214)

Books that he authored or coauthored include: *The De-velopment of Consciousness—A Confluent Theory of Values,*[18] *Developing Human Values,*[19] *The Genesis Effect—Personal and Organizational Transformation,*[20] *and Values Shift—A Guide to Personal and Organiza-tional Transformation.*[21] They neatly explain how a person's capabilities and values change as one advances in consciousness from early childhood on through adolescence and adulthood. His books offer clear insights into human growth and behavior and are appealing to laymen and professionals alike.

★★

Future Psychological Principles

Tour Guide's Commentary:

Another basic principle of human nature is that the human mind is complex and can be described in a variety of ways. These gallery tours are not all-inclusive. There are additional realms of thought for this tour guide to explore. There are other notable psychologists who have identified additional principles of human nature that can and perhaps should be applied when endeavoring to understand another person. As those principles are encountered, tour participants are encouraged to include them with the repertoire of principles that have been explained along this tour.

Similarly, it is important to consider that the science of Psychology like most sciences will surely advance. New principles will forever be introduced in the future. As they are introduced and validated, they will deserve to also be included in this same repertoire.

Notes:

1. Milton Rokeach, *Beliefs, Attitudes and Values: A Theory of Organization and Change*, Jossey-Bass Inc Pub (June 1, 1968). ISBN-10: 087589013X, ISBN-13: 978-0875890135

2. Milton Rokeach, *The Nature of Human Values*, Free Press (August 1, 1973). ISBN-10: 0029267501, ISBN-13: 978-0029267509

3. Michael Doyle and David Straus, *How to Make Meetings Work, The New Interaction Method.* Berkley Trade—Mass Market Paperback Reprint (September 1, 1993), ISBN-10: 0425138704, ISBN-13: 978-0425138700

4. Lavinia Hall, Editor, *Negotiation—Strategies for Mutual Gain, The Basic Seminar of the Harvard Program on Negotiation,* with Section 3 titled *Facilitated Collaborative Problem Solving and Process Management,* contributed by David Straus. Sage Publications Inc. (June 24, 1992), ISBN-10: 0803948506, ISBN-13: 978-0803948501

5. Johnson O'Connor, *Understanding Your Aptitudes*, by the Writing Committee of the Johnson O'Connor Research Foundation. At the time of this composition, a free download is available from the foundation's website www.jocrf.org

6. Margaret E. Broadley, *Your Natural Gifts—How to recognize and develop them for success and self-fulfillment,* Epm Pubns Inc; 3rd edition (August 1, 1991), ISBN-10: 0939009560, ISBN-13: 978-0939009565. (As explained on the foundation's website, Margaret Broadley was a personal friend of Johnson O'Connor. In this book she relates her ideas and perspective about his work and philosophy, as well as about aptitudes, careers, occupational patterns, and the importance of vocabulary.)

7. Carl G. Jung, *Psychological Types (The Collected Works of C.G. Jung, Vol. 6) (Bollinger Series XX)*, Princeton University Press (October 1, 1976), ISBN-10: 0691018138, ISBN-13: 978-0691018133

8. Carl G. Jung, *The Archetypes and The Collective Unconscious (The Collected Works of C.G.Jung, Vol. 9 Part 1),* Princeton University Press; 2nd ed. Edition (August 1, 1981), ISBN-10: 0691018332, ISBN-13: 978-0691018331

9. Noreen Monroe Guzie and Tad Guzie, *About Men & Women: How Your Masculine and Feminine Archetypes Shape Your Destiny. Understanding Your Personality, Goals, Relationships & Stages of Life. A Complement to the Psychological Types.* Enlightenment Publications, L.L.C.; 2nd edition (June 10, 2016), ISBN-10: 0997204206, ISBN-13: 978-0997204209

10. Kenneth Bullmer, *The Art of Empathy: A Manual for Improving Accuracy of Interpersonal Perception*, Human Sciences Press; 1st Edition (June 1, 1975), ISBN-10: 087705228X, ISBN-13: 978-0877052289

11. Isabel Briggs Myers, *Gifts Differing: Understanding Personality Type*, with her son Peter B. Myers, Consulting Psychologists Press, Reprint Edition (January 1995), ISBN-10: 089106074X, ISBN-13: 978-0891060741

12. David Kiersey, *Please Understand Me: Character and Temperament Types*, coauthored with Marilyn Bates, B & D Books; 5th edition (November 1, 1984), ISBN-10: 0960695400, ISBN-13: 978-0960695409

13. David Kiersey, *Please Understand Me II: Temperament, Character, Intelligence*, Prometheus Nemesis Book Co; 1st Edition (May 1, 1998), ISBN-10: 1885705026, ISBN-13: 978-1885705020

14. Elton B. McNeil, *Human Socialization*, Brooks/Cole Publishing Co. (August 1969), ISBN-10: 0818581956, ISBN-13: 978-0818581953

15. George Kaluger and Meriem Fair Kaluger, *Human Development: The Span of Life*, Mosby: 2nd Edition (May 1979), ISBN-10: 0801626102, ISBN-13: 978-0801626104

16. Stanley Greenspan, *The Growth of the Mind: And the Endangered Origins of Intelligence*, with Beryl Lieff Benderly, Da Capo Press (October 9, 1998), ISBN-10: 0738200263, ISBN-13: 978-0738200262

17. Stanley Greenspan, *Building Healthy Minds: The Six Experiences That Create Intelligence And Emotional Growth In Babies And Young Children*, with Nancy Breslau Lewis, Da Capo Press (October 1. 2000), ISBN-10: 0738203564, ISBN-13: 978-0738203560

18. Brian P. Hall, *The Development of Consciousness—A Confluent Theory of Values*, Paulist Press (1976), ISBN-10: 0809118947, ISBN-13: 978-0809118946

19. Brian P. Hall, *Developing Human Values*, coauthored with Bruce Taylor, Janet Kalvin and Larry S. Rosen, International Values Institute of Marian College (September 1, 1990), ISBN-10: 1879494019, ISBN-13: 978-1879494015

20. Brian P. Hall, *The Genesis Effect: Personal and Organizational Transformations*, Wipf & Stock Pub (August 1, 2006), ISBN-10: 1597527025, ISBN-13: 978-1597527026

21. Brian P. Hall, *Values Shift: A Guide to Personal and Organizational Transformation*, Resource Publications (August 1, 2006), ISBN-10: 1597526908, ISBN-13: 978-1597526906

Gallery of the
World Chess Game Academy

The Third Session
Life Strategies

Tour Guide's Introduction:

As explained earlier, this third session focuses upon human strategies. In terms of chess game analogies, this is a study of *how* people play their games of life to win that which they desire, within the limits of their movement abilities.

Unlike previous galleries in which various word-paintings were on display with accompanying written interpretations, this portion of our tour is different in that we are about to enter a lecture hall, take a seat, relax a little, and listen to (read) an explanation of this particular subject. ☺ The title of this presentation is *Life Strategies.* It now proceeds as follows:

One appealing reason for acquiring the ability to understand life strategies is that people become more interesting when we can comprehend their game plans for attaining whatever it is that they desire in life. We can then view them as chess people moving about to various positions on the world chessboard. As they implement their strategies for attainment they experience both successes and failures, both of which are emotional and therefore dramatic. We can therefore also view them as players enacting the dramas of their lives on the world stage as Shakespeare so eloquently described. Once we have this ability to comprehend the underlying reasons for

219

people's actions and the dramatic situations they encounter, we will be pleased to discover that no person anywhere will ever again be boring! Even those who are seemingly quiet and inactive will become interesting as we seek to understand the underlying reasons for their inactivity. Everywhere we go we will become intrigued with the life dramas that we see people enacting all around us on the world stage. ☺

With an understanding of *life strategies* we can more easily analyze people's options for playing their life games. We can also more easily determine what their courses of action are likely to be. In addition, if we are so interested, we can more easily determine if it is feasible to help them enhance their strategies in return for their willingness to help us enhance ours. This comes back to the concept of engaging in equal value exchanges between two mutually interested individuals, as discussed earlier on this tour, both in terms of physical and mental (emotional) value.

Admittedly, this preceding concept of exploring for mutual value exchange opportunities has a selfish connotation. It is to be noted that there are enlightened individuals who have the perceptive ability to see the *good* in another person regardless of her supposed problems and faults. As a result such an enlightened person may make an effort to help the other individual even though she has nothing of apparent value to offer in return. However, the enlightened person does experience personal satisfaction for having helped someone and this is of significant mental (emotional) value. It is to be noted that it takes an exceptionally perceptive person to see and appreciate the inner beauty of certain people. Those who can are skilled in the art of empathy and likely live on a higher level of consciousness, to be explained later on this tour.

In the case of certain individuals who happen to have certain values that appeal to us, we may become especially interested in which values we might have to offer them that would be appealing, with the hope that an exchange can be arranged. As we engage in these determinations we will strive to see the world chessboard from the perspectives of others, along with their movement abilities, the strategies they employ in playing their games of life, and what forms of value we might be able to offer them that could aid in their advancement. This again IS a key element of EMPATHY, the *life skill* that this academy endeavors to teach.

Again, the overall objective of this third session is to further explain the concept of life strategies. While it is one thing to understand the concept, *how* to go about the actual recognition of another person's use of them is the subject matter of the forthcoming fourth session.

As we endeavor to study the nature of human strategies, it is important to realize that there are probably as many of them as there are people on this planet. Hence, it is not possible to define every single strategy that a person might utilize because there are too many. However, with the aid of *examples,* it is possible to acquire a basic understanding of strategic concepts. Hence, as a means of conceptual explanation, a series of typical *example strategies* is provided in this third session.

As a matter of interest, many of us may also be in the process of establishing or refining our own life strategies. Hence a review of the examples in this section can serve another purpose, namely that of how they might be applied to aid in our personal advancements toward whichever goals we may be seeking.

Broadly speaking, examples of life strategies can be explained with the use of the following world chessboard analogies:

Starting Positions, Mental and Physical

Destination Positions, Mental and Physical

Techniques for advancing from Starting Positions to Destination Positions.

Please note the distinction between mental and physical. It is important to realize that one's personal happiness and satisfaction with life is dependent upon one's *state of mind*. It is easy to conceive of a person advancing from one physical location to another on the world chessboard. However, each and every person is also challenged to advance to a position where mental (emotional) satisfaction is achieved. Such mental advancement can be as challenging as physical advancement, and possibly more so.

Physical Starting Positions

A person's physical starting position is usually visible and therefore easy to determine, such as where she lives, works, travels, attends school, etc.

Mental Starting Positions

A person's mental starting position can be thought of as her present mental structure. This includes her array of mental characteristics in the form of aptitudes, skills, psychological type, archetype, beliefs, opinions, knowledge, etc. With an understanding of those characteristics as explained in the second session, it then becomes possible to recognize them in the many people we observe in action on the world stage. Through observation and listening along with a little practice, one can over time form conclusions about how those mental characteristics are manifested in another person.

Physical Destination Positions

As with physical starting positions, physical destination positions are easy to describe, however they are not as easy to determine because they pertain to another person's internal visions of the future, and those visions are not externally visible to others. Wherever a person would like to advance in this world along with whichever material possessions she would like to acquire comprise her physical destination positions. They include desirable career positions in particular locations, comfortable living conditions, and the accumulation of material wealth in either in modest or more elaborate form.

Mental Destination Positions

Similarly, a person's mental destination positions exist as inner visions within her mind and are not externally visible to others. They may include visions of desirable family situations that she would like to experience where there is peace, harmony, love and happiness. They may include visions of desirable social situations in which she is highly regarded by a certain group or type of people, possibly those with significant social status. They may also include visions of desirable career situations with personal satisfactions for certain accomplishments. They can also include more complex visions that can admittedly be a major challenge to determine and understand.

Vague and Unknown Destination Positions

It is to be noted that many people do not have clear destination positions in mind. Some are still trying to determine where they wish to advance in life, hence their present goal or destination is to somehow clarify their objectives, possibly with the aid of suitable counselors or mentors. Others are afflicted with negative opinions about themselves and have no intention of ever establishing any particular destination. Their chosen life strategy may be to aimlessly wander along and follow whichever *pathways of least resistance* lie before them.

It is also to be noted that if these same individuals were to somehow recognize what valuable aptitudes lie in the depths of their mentalities, they could then recognize that the development of impressive personal skills are indeed possible for them. They could then become convinced that pathways to success do exist and that they have the means to favorably impress a multitude of people. As a result their entire outlook on life could change.

Example Strategies for Advancement from Starting to Destination Positions, both Mental and Physical

Strategy of Acquiring *Aptitude Assurance*:

Acquiring *Aptitude Assurance* is a first step toward the pursuit of a goal. A starting point for any person on the pathway of life is to somehow acquire enough self-confidence to be assured of the following:

She indeed HAS potential in the form of valuable mental aptitudes. No matter what anyone might have said to the contrary, no matter what sort of negative experiences she may have encountered in the past, in spite of all that, she still has valuable aptitudes within her mentality, no matter how hidden they may presently be.

These aptitudes CAN be developed into useful skills.

These skills WILL enable her to experience both social and career success. This includes the financial means to live in physical comfort, and the social ability to comfortably interact with family and friends.

The irony here is that one is at a loss to implement this strategy if one has no awareness or understanding of the concept. Some type of outside intervention may be needed. Somehow every person needs to be awakened to this core principle of human nature.

Of course, an excellent way to be assured that one has valuable inner aptitudes is to actually discover them. This leads to the next strategy for consideration.

Strategy of Aptitude Discovery:

Once a person is convinced that she has been born with valuable aptitudes that can be developed into useful skills, she will naturally become curious to discover what these aptitudes happen to be. To satisfy this curiosity a person can implement a *Strategy of Aptitude Discovery*. This is not as difficult as it may first appear to be. Essentially, one can take either of two approaches for implementation: One can seek professional counseling, which may entail a significant financial investment. Or, one can take a "do-it-yourself" approach that is inexpensive and affordable for virtually everyone.

As just mentioned, if one has the financial means, one can discover her natural aptitudes with the aid of professional counselors that can administer tests that are designed for this purpose. These counselors can also offer assistance with interpreting test results. Sometimes such services are provided free of charge as part of the guidance programs within certain school systems, especially schools and institutions of advanced learning.

225

Realizing that many people do not have access to professional counseling services, there is also an inexpensive "do-it-yourself" approach for discovering one's internal aptitudes. One can utilize the internet to visit the website of a popular bookseller and then do a keyword search, using such keywords as "aptitude" or "career planning". Various suggested books will then appear from which to choose.

As an example, one particular book on this exact subject is titled *Discover What You're Best At – The Complete Career System that Let's You Test Yourself to Discover Your Own True Career Capabilities,* by Linda Gale.[1] As explained on that book's back cover: "The book's unique National Career Aptitude System enables you to identify not only your interests but also your innate talents and potential skills, and then to match your career strengths to dozens of more than 1,100 jobs described in detail." Linda Gale is the coauthor of four career books. This book, *Discover What You're Best At...,* provides an excellent opportunity for virtually everyone to inexpensively discover their natural aptitudes, and is therefore recommended.

After a person discovers her natural aptitudes and to her amazement finds them to be quite appealing, she will then need to implement *Strategies of Skill Development* that are based upon utilizing those natural aptitudes as starting points.

Strategies of Skill Development:

An obvious strategy for skill development is an educational plan of action to qualify a person for a chosen career position, one that utilizes her natural aptitudes. Ideally, such a plan is made with the aid of a qualified counselor, or a team of them. Again, if no such guidance is available, inexpensive guide books are available.

Educational importance requires little additional emphasis or explanation since it is already obvious to virtually everyone. It is mentioned here because it is crucial and therefore deserves to be included in this listing of example strategies.

Strategy of *Developing Communication Skills:*

This is a beginning and basic strategy for advancement to virtually anywhere. No matter what a person's objectives may be in either her personal or career life, she will need the admiration, respect, appreciation, and cooperation of others in order to succeed. This will entail the use of effective communication skills.

It is easy for a person to assume that she knows how to communicate because she has been conversing with others all throughout her life. At the same time, it is amazing how much more effective one can become with additional training and practice.

For a person who wishes to be an especially effective communicator, she can engage in an ongoing self-improvement program. This does not need to be laborious. Interesting books are available that explain the principles of effective communication that are also enjoyable to read. One does need to practice the principles they explain in order to achieve their benefits. However, trying out the various techniques that they describe can also be interesting and fun. Such a self-inspired and self-planned program can become a life-long hobby, a spare-time activity in other words. Among the resulting benefits can also be increased self-confidence in one's abilities.

For any person who is interested in such a self-study program, numerous books are available that can be located through any of the conventional booksellers. It is suggested that one begin with those books that teach basic techniques which are easily applied in social situations as well as in educational and career environments. Then, to become even more effective, it is suggested that one proceed to a more comprehensive text that delves into the underlying theories of effective communication. Following are a few examples:

Two enjoyable books that teach basic principles are:

1. *Conversationally Speaking: Tested Ways to Improve Your Personal and Social Effectiveness* by Alan Garner. McGraw-Hill Education; 3rd edition (April 22, 1997). ISBN-10: 1565656296, ISBN-13: 978-1565656291
2. *The Art of Conversation: Change Your Life with Confident Communication* by Judy Apps. Capstone; 1 edition (June 3, 2014). ISBN-10: 0857085387, ISBN-13: 978-0857085382

A great text that delves into the underlying theories of effective communication and how they can be applied happens to be a college textbook:

Communicating Effectively by Saundra Hybels and Richard Weaver II. McGraw-Hill Education; 11 edition (March 27, 2014). ISBN-10: 0073523879, ISBN-13: 978-0073523873

Quoting from one bookseller's on-line description of this text:

"*Communicating Effectively* presents a comprehensive introduction to interpersonal, intercultural, professional, group, and public communication. Providing just the right amount of theory and research, the book is packed with thought-provoking prose and activities that engage student interest. A pragmatic approach enables students to appreciate ideas, concepts, and theories in their own lives."

It is important to remember that effective communication entails having an understanding of those with whom one is conversing, and how best to relate with them. *This entails the use of empathic skills, for which this book endeavors to offer insights and techniques.*

Strategy of *Employing the Golden Rule*:

This is another beginning and basic strategy for advancement to virtually anywhere. It is important to remember that throughout life it will always be necessary to contribute value to others in exchange for receiving value from them. This is a basic application of the *Golden Rule,* namely to do unto others as one would like them to do unto oneself, or words to that effect. Therefore, in any endeavor one attempts, one's planning must always entail a strategy of contributing equally for what one desires with the objective of achieving a "win-win" outcome. Clarifications of this strategy and ideas for its implementation are provided at various points along these gallery tours.

In discussing this strategy it is almost impossible to overemphasize the importance of contributing mental (emotional) value to others, particularly in the form of sincere recognition when and where it is appropriate to do so. This is explained in more detail in the *Gallery of Friendship and Recognition* in Part 4 of this book. However, it will help to advance a few basic principles here: To give someone insincere recognition in the form of a phony compliment is far worse than no recognition at all. Most people can intuitively sense such insincerity and be easily repelled as a result. To instead appropriately give someone sincere praise that is based upon accurate recognition of the person's actual positive attributes is a real skill. This entails an

229

ability to recognize and appreciate the person's capabilities along with what it took to develop them. It also entails an ability to recognize the value that a person contributes to others, especially altruistic value that benefits others without receiving any monetary value in return. It also helps if this recognition is for certain admirable qualities that are not obvious to others. To instead offer a compliment that is no more than a statement of the obvious will not be nearly as appreciated. Here again, the ability to recognize and appreciate the inner depths and admirable qualities of another person requires the development and use of empathic skills.

Strategy of *Obtaining Ongoing Career Advice:*

Just as it is helpful to obtain qualified advice for the establishment of starting and destination points, it can be helpful to obtain ongoing advice on a regular basis through the course of one's career. For such a purpose it can be helpful to have a mentor, also as explained at various points along these gallery tours.

Strategy of *Participation in Professional Groups or Societies:*

Members of certain professions often have certain societies unique to their profession that they can join. Membership in such a group enables one to meet and befriend people of the same profession from other organizations. Having multiple contacts within other organizations can be especially helpful when and if one needs to make a job change. They can alert one to possible opportunities within their organizations, and also be available as helpful references.

Strategy of *Developing a Brave Attitude:*

This is another beginning and basic strategy for advancement to virtually anywhere. A person needs to *believe* in herself and her inherent abilities in order to advance, to attain meaningful positions on the board, whatever they may be. This may require mental bravery and possibly a lot of it, especially if one happens to be living in an environment of negative influences, which unfortunately is the case for many. After determining one's aptitudes, psychological type and archetype, and after realizing that one *can* develop meaningful communication skills, one awakens to the fact that she is capable of major advancements across the world chessboard to meaningful positions. At the same time, one may be living in the midst of people who have no such ambitions, and worse yet may be inclined to discourage a person with a continual bombardment of negative opinions. Such people may even go so far as to ridicule those who attempt to advance. It is amazing how the negative attitudes of others can undermine one's self confidence and thereby inhibit one's advancement. It can therefore require major mental bravery to truly believe in oneself and one's inherent abilities in the midst of such adversity. A strategy for developing a strong, brave attitude with true belief in oneself is therefore needed.

One of the best strategies is to seek reinforcement from respectable people such as teachers, counselors, and mentors. One can share her self-assessments with these people along with one's ambitions. Their approval and encouragement can go a long way toward strengthening one's self-confidence and assuring one of her self-worth. In addition, such individuals will often help a person plan effective strategies for advancement. These same teachers, counselors, and/or mentors can also benefit themselves with feelings of emotional satisfaction for having helped someone.

When doing self-assessments and seeking advice, it is important to not sell oneself short. A person can have more potential than she first realizes. One can sometimes be advised to set mediocre goals that are beneath one's abilities. It is better to set one's goals high, strive to advance as far as possible, and then be pleased with whatever one manages to achieve. The alternative is to set mediocre goals and settle for the achievement of something that is beneath one's actual capabilities, resulting in a life of dissatisfaction.

Along these same lines and as with seeking medical advice, it can be helpful to seek second, third, and possibly more opinions. This is because no single adviser is likely to have all the right insights and answers.

Strategy of *Learning by Doing:*

Another strategy is to simply *dive in* and get started with something, no matter how scary a certain pathway looks, and no matter what any negative person has to say. After all, negative people really don't count. Who needs them? Why not simply walk out of their lives? It is okay to do so quietly without further disturbing them. One who actually employs this strategy of *diving in* and getting started is often surprised to discover that the experience is far easier than she first anticipated, especially if she has been practicing the *Golden Rule.* This of course leads to enhanced bravery and self-confidence.

Strategy of *Expecting and Appreciating Mistakes:*

It is also helpful to consider that mistakes will be made, but at the same time every mistake is a learning experience. One of the ironies of life is that people who have learned through mistakes are often more qualified for advancement than those who have not had the benefit of such learning experience. There are some supposedly capable people who travel a fast track upward while making few if any mistakes along the way. When they finally do make a major mistake, which virtually every person does sooner or later, they can be mentally devastated and sometimes emotionally incapacitated. On the other hand, those who have made mistakes early in life and worked their way through them are often better equipped to deal with more serious complications later in life, which for most people usually do occur. Therefore, it is worth considering a strategy of *charging in* and trying something that is appealing, with the realization that complications may occur. Also, remember that the consequences of one's mistakes can be easier to deal with if one has had good intentions and has been practicing the *Golden Rule.* This is because when mistakes are made, one often does need the friendship and cooperation of others to help resolve them.

Strategy of *Successive Positions:*

Many positions require that a person have previous forms of experience in order to qualify for advancement. Therefore, when a person makes it her goal to attain a certain position, she may need to first advance through a sequence of prior positions to acquire the necessary experience.

A common example of advancing through a series of positions to a more advanced position is commonly seen in government.

While there are always exceptions, in the United States a common pathway is from a city government position to a state government position. From there, a select few will strive for a congressional position. From there, a still more select few will strive for one of the top executive positions. The same approach is often used in corporate situations where people strive for advancement to ever higher tiers of management. (Of course, as with many ideas there are always *exceptions to the rule.*)

No matter what a person's career goals may be, realistic or idealistic, it may be necessary to first set intermediate goals that will thereby provide one with the experience needed to qualify for more advanced objectives.

Strategy of *Gaining Experience through Voluntary Activities:*

Career advancement often requires that one somehow acquire necessary experience to qualify for such advancement. If one has an interest in the services of a certain charity or volunteer organization, one may then wish to participate. Often such organizations are in need of volunteer leadership, which could thereby provide a person with valuable managerial experience.

Strategy of *Maintaining Personal Health and Physical Fitness:*

While virtually every person is already aware of this, considering the importance this matter, it deserves to be included in this listing of example strategies.

Virtually every person would like to maintain her physical health and personal appearance. The importance of a physical exercise program cannot be overemphasized. Participation in some type of health club works well for some people. There are many other methods for obtaining regular exercise, examples of which most people are already aware.

Strategy of *Seeking Like Mindedness:*

Here is an example strategy that may forever be open to debate:

It is fairly well understood that between men and women, opposites often attract. However, over time their opposite characteristics can sometimes become annoying to each other when and if they marry. Many counselors will suggest that like-mindedness is a key ingredient for mental harmony between couples, along with perhaps a few opposite characteristics that can serve as points of desirable fascination between them.

Sometimes there are social groups that cater to a certain interest, examples of which might be sports activities, book discussions, hobbies, etc. If one has a certain interest and joins a social group pertaining to that interest, there is a chance of meeting likeminded people within that group who share the same interests.

As most are aware, there are now various online internet services that match people on the basis of similar interests and personalities. There can be both pros and cons to such services. One of the pros is that one can indeed meet a wonderful like-minded person with this approach. One of the cons is that one can also can come into direct contact with problem people from virtually any segment of society. Careful personal judgment needs to be utilized.

Strategy of *Seeking Mutual Understanding and Support:*

Here is an example strategy for seeking like mindedness that can spark both humor and criticism (not to mention *alarm* in the minds of certain men) : ☺

It may be appropriate for a woman to assertively take a man for a proverbial "walk in the park on a Sunday afternoon" and ask him some *down to earth* serious questions like: "What exactly is your career destination, and how do you plan to achieve it?" She might also challenge him with a statement like: "Prove to me that you actually have the capability!" Her underlying motive might rightly be to determine if he can actually be a good provider, which of course is of extreme importance, especially if they ever have children. If she happens to have career interests of her own, she might also ask him to explain how he will encourage and support *her* career interests. For some men with real romantic interests, such assertiveness on the part of a woman can be a real *wake-up call* to get serious about career planning and implementation (especially if those men really like what they see). ☺

It may also be appropriate for two people to silently ask of the other these questions: "Do you have the social poise and ability to impress my family, friends, and career associates?" "Can you harmoniously fit in and interact with them?" "Might you consider enhancing your communication skills and developing your empathic abilities? Believe it or not, I have just the book for you to read. Here it is!" ☺

While this next comment may appear to be a statement of the obvious, it deserves to be included here: It is also appropriate for people to ask each other about their future aspirations in terms of family, home, recreational interests, social interests, etc. If one person dreams of living in a mansion and being a world traveler with no children to slow her down, while the other dreams of having a house full of kids in a modest urban environment, there may be problems. ☺

Strategy for *Appropriate Child Rearing:*

Dr. Stanley Greenspan, to whom a tribute has been offered in a previous gallery, was a pediatrician who wrote various eye-opening books in regard to human development. Two in particular that deserve mention here are:

Growth of the Mind – And the Endangered Origins of Intelligence[2]

Building Healthy Minds – The Six Experiences that Create Intelligence and Emotional Growth in Babies and Young Children[3]

As virtually every parent will attest, the healthy mental development of children is an art and science all in itself. Following the advice recommended in Dr. Greenspan's books would be a rewarding worthwhile endeavor, and a strategy all in itself.

Strategy for *Achieving Inner Peace and Contentment:*

In the midst of a busy, demanding, challenging, and often chaotic life, there is often a need to take a break and reassess one's life along with the issues one is facing. Everyone has a need to periodically relax and experience inner peace and contentment. Here is where the inspiration and support from the Master Artists can be of help. This is explained in greater detail in Part 4 of these tours, in the *Gallery of Inner Inspiration.*

Strategy of *Establishing Dual Destination Positions - Both Idealistic and Realistic:*

Some individuals may discover that their mental characteristics are a match for certain idealistic careers. Examples might be those of a movie star, professional athlete, or maybe an astronaut. Realizing that a fortunate few will actually achieve these idealistic positions, it is perfectly fine to pursue them and have fun in the process. Also realizing that only a few of those positions are actually available, it is important to simultaneously pursue career positions that are more numerous and therefore more easily attainable, and also have fun in the process. There is wisdom in establishing dual or multiple career destinations, one that is idealistic and one or several that are more realistic. If the idealistic position is reached, one can rejoice. If instead a more realistic position is reached, one can still rejoice.

An example could be that of a music student who confides to her teacher that her goal is to someday be a concert pianist. Her teacher, blessed with many years of wisdom, might reply by saying: "Great! Go for it! But be sure to enroll in a double major. Obtain your music teaching certificate besides." ☺

Strategy of *Establishing Career Destinations in Specific Geographic Areas:*

Some individuals are receptive to geographic relocation. Others have specific preferences such as the same area where they grew up where they will remain close to family and friends. If one has a specific geographic preference, it is important to establish a career destination for which opportunities exist within that preferred geographic area.

Strategy of *Establishing Career Destinations with Alternate Opportunities:*

Using the field of engineering as an example, there are opportunities for civil engineers in virtually every city and county. Their career duties at these various locations can be quite similar, hence their career experience is transferable if they wish to make a job change. On the other hand, mechanical and electrical engineers can sometimes become overly specialized in a single product area, for which there may only be one or two manufacturers in an entire country. Then, if a problem develops with their employer, they sometimes have few alternate opportunities where their prior career experience applies. As a result, they can remain *stuck* where they are and become very miserable. While specialized careers may be appealing, it may be advantageous to instead select a career that is more sought after by various alternate employers in one's desired geographical area.

Strategy of *Advance Inside-Research:*

If a certain organization is appealing from the outside, it can be helpful to obtain an inside view by meeting with one or more employees within that organization, to be sure they are pleased to be working there. If their reports are positive, one has added assurance. If they instead describe certain internal problems, there may then be reason to seriously consider alternatives.

Thus concludes our series of *example strategies.* As explained at the beginning of this 3rd session, there are an infinite number of different strategies that people may employ to achieve their destination goals. While it is not possible to explain all of them, a conceptual understanding can be obtained with the aid of basic examples as have just been provided. One can then more easily recognize the orientation of another person's life in terms of the following:

Starting points, mental and physical

Destination points, mental and physical

Strategies for advancement from one to the other

239

Tour Guide's Commentary:

As explained above, the purpose for this 3rd session at the World Chess Game Academy has been to explain the concept of life strategies, with the aid of chess game analogies. *How* to recognize the strategies that a person utilizes in her life to obtain that which she desires is the subject of the forthcoming 4th session.

Notes:

1. Linda Gale, *Discover What You're Best At,* Touchstone; 21st Revised ed. Edition (August 10, 1998), ISBN-10: 0684839563, ISBN-13: 978-0684839561

2. Stanley Greenspan, *The Growth of the Mind: And the Endangered Origins of Intelligence*, with Beryl Lieff Benderly, Da Capo Press (October 9, 1998), ISBN-10: 0738200263, ISBN-13: 978-0738200262

3. Stanley Greenspan, *Building Healthy Minds: The Six Experiences That Create Intelligence And Emotional Growth In Babies And Young Children*, with Nancy Breslau Lewis, Da Capo Press (October 1. 2000), ISBN-10: 0738203564, ISBN-13: 978-0738203560

Gallery of the
World Chess Game Academy

The Fourth Session
Detective Skills

Tour Guide's Introduction:

As mentioned earlier, when people engage in their life games on the world chessboard they are simultaneously enacting the dramas of their lives on the world stage. Therefore, this fourth session of the curriculum focuses on the development of *detective skills* with which to interpret the many dramas that are being enacted right before our eyes every day by the many people we encounter. Throughout this session as in various others you will notice a degree of repetition as certain key concepts are viewed from a new perspective to further emphasize their importance.

As with the third session, we will again enter a lecture hall, take a seat, relax a little, and listen to (read) an explanation of this particular subject, which now begins as follows:

As we become detectives we will have a keen interest in observing people's *actions* on the world stage, and in listening to their *dialogs* with various individuals. Actions and dialog will provide us with the *clues* we need to determine what a person values in life and what he is attempting to achieve, along with his abilities and strategies for attainment.

Every *clue* that can be derived becomes a *piece to a puzzle.* When enough pieces are gathered they can be put together to form *pic-*

tures that fit into two categories: *still-life* pictures that depict what a person values in life, and *motion pictures* that depict what a person is doing to obtain those values. Another way of saying this is that the still-life pictures depict what a person *desires*, and the motion pictures depict his *strategies* for attainment, which might also be called his *game plans of action.*

However, before we can assemble these puzzle pieces into pictures, we must first find them. Once again, we must therefore become *detectives* in search of *clues* that will reveal those pieces. To be proficient detectives we need to have an understanding of *which clues* to search for. These are about to be defined in the form of *questions* that can be *silently* asked about whomever we wish to better understand. *Answers* to these silent questions can then be provided to us as we employ our soon to be acquired observation and listening skills.

It is to be noted that the answers to our *clue questions* will likely be provided in a somewhat random order, depending upon whatever a person of interest happens to be doing and discussing whenever we happen to be observing and listening. When enough of these random pieces have been gathered it will then be our challenge to assemble them together into meaningful pictures. As you can see, this is similar to solving a conventional jigsaw puzzle in which a container of randomly mixed pieces is provided and the solver is challenged to assemble them into a picture. Unlike a jigsaw puzzle, the pieces must first be found; they are not immediately provided in a neat container. Also unlike a jigsaw puzzle where the completed picture is often provided on the outside of the container, no immediate picture is provided to show what the final result should look like. Another complication is that one is also challenged to assemble mental-motion pictures which depict life strategies in addition to still-life pictures which depict life desires. ☺

It is fitting to again provide a cautionary note that begins with the familiar phrase: "Rome was not built in a day!" Many pictures that you create will not be completed in a day either. Time will be needed to first find the pieces and then assemble them into meaningful pictures. If you already know someone well, someone with whom you have frequent contact for example, the entire process may be fast and easy. However, for those with whom you have only occasional contact, you will have fewer opportunities to find the right clues. More time will therefore be needed—maybe weeks, months, or even years. It is also to be noted that people change over time. In particular, they normally become more mature as they grow older, and thereby become wiser through the benefits of additional learning experiences. Therefore, the pictures that you create will also change over time as the person evolves and becomes more mature. Especially for those people with whom you have only limited contact, some degree of patience will be needed.

Before becoming too discouraged with the complexity of these puzzles, it is important to consider that this entire process can be enjoyable, and actually rather intriguing. Think of the fun you had as a child drawing and coloring pictures. Anyone who likes to solve puzzles or dabble in art (which is just about everyone) can find this creative mental imagery to be a pleasing ongoing pastime.

Much of the information presented in the second and third sessions was in reference to world chessboard analogies in which movement abilities and strategies for attainment were discussed. As noted earlier, it is when people attempt to implement their strategies on the world *chessboard* that they encounter their *dramas of life* on the world *stage*. As is about to be explained in this fourth session, an understanding of *world stage analogies* is an especially helpful tool for developing one's detective skills.

243

A basic premise underlying the information to be presented is that every single action that a person ever takes is for the acquirement of value in one form or another. This can be mental value (the desire for some form of emotional satisfaction) or physical value (the desire to live in some form of physical comfort). Such actions either succeed or fail, causing a person to experience emotional feelings that range from pleasing to displeasing, or desirable to undesirable. It is the pursuit of human values with associated successes and failures and resulting emotional feelings of pleasure and pain that make a person's life dramatic.

Every person's life is a *unique dramatic adventure story*. Hence, the story of every person's life could be written in the form of an adventure novel. Such a novel could have many individual chapters covering the many interesting incidents, events, trials, tribulations, challenges, successes, and failures that the person encountered during the course of his life. As already explained, every person's novel life is enacted as a fascinating drama on the world stage, as William Shakespeare has so eloquently described.

The settings for any person's dramatic life story can be virtually anywhere, a quiet place in the countryside perhaps, maybe in a busy city, possibly on a battlefield, or anywhere else. Similarly, a person's life story can take place on any level of society. The characters in a person's life story can be peasants in a lower echelon, kings and queens in an upper echelon, or anyone in between.

Every person's story without exception revolves around the pursuit of personal *desires or values* of one form or another. Stated differently, throughout every person's life is the desire for various forms of *life satisfaction.* These include opportunities to participate in *interesting and pleasing activities,* some of which are as follows:

Interesting Conversation

Social Activities

Recreational Activities

Making Friends

Finding Romance

Falling in Love

Intimacy

Raising a Family

Family Gatherings

Fun Vacations

Fascinating Travel

Entertainment

Artistic Creation

Athletic Accomplishment

Academic Accomplishment

Career Advancement and Success

Business Development and Success

Financial Security

Personal Safety

Solving Problems

Overcoming Adversity

Overcoming Poverty

Overcoming Physical Deficiencies

Aiding the Disadvantaged

Helping Others

Guiding Others

Leading Others

Creative Contributions

Achieving Mental Peace and Harmony

Contributing to World Peace and Harmony

And, the list goes on!

Once again, every person's life story is actually an intriguing dramatic novel with a sequence of chapters that progress from scene to scene throughout the person's life on the world stage as he strives to obtain and experience that which he desires, namely his chosen values.

As in virtually every novel, there is rarely an easy pathway to personal satisfaction and happiness. If there were, the novel would be boring and the reader would lose interest. Instead, through the course of their lives as people strive for desirable experiences they encounter problems, obstacles, challenges and adversities. As a result, a meaningful part of every person's life story pertains to the challenges of solving problems and overcoming obstacles. In many cases, this entails the acquirement of additional skills. It is the problems they encounter and their efforts to overcome them that make people interesting to observe. That is what makes their life stories especially fascinating to follow.

As we become *detectives* and search for *clues* to comprehend people's life stories, it is important to keep a few underlying *principles* in mind, some of which have been previously described:

246

Every desirable activity that any person pursues in life provides him with some form of *value*, either mental or physical. Mental value is often associated with some form of emotional satisfaction. Physical value is often associated with something that has monetary worth.

Every person is required to contribute some form of value in exchange for whatever value he desires to receive in return. If he is unable to do this, he will usually be "out of luck." Therefore, a portion of a person's life is often devoted to acquiring value that can be used for contribution or exchange purposes, in order to receive desirable value in return. Prime examples include the acquirement of an education, a career, occupational experience, monetary resources, physical attractiveness, interpersonal communication skills, empathic abilities, etc.

To reemphasize, people are hesitant, reluctant, and often completely unwilling to contribute value to others unless they can receive some form of desirable value in return. Here is an underlying reason for personal problems, namely that people lack the values that they need to contribute, in order to receive in return the values that they desire from others, either in emotional or monetary form.

Every exchange of value between individuals, whether it is mental or physical, has a variation of three possible emotional outcomes: "win-win" when both are pleased, "win-lose" when one is pleased and the other is displeased, or "lose-lose" when both are displeased. Those who practice the *Golden Rule* and focus on "win-win" strategies are the most likely to experience satisfaction in life.

Based upon the preceding review of various underlying issues in people's basic *life stories*, we will now acquaint ourselves with several series of *example clue questions*. These examples plus additional questions that we formulate on our own will combine to form a ***mental repertoire of clue questions*** to reside in the backs of our minds.   These are questions that we will silently ask ourselves about others but for which we will normally not have immediate answers.   Instead, we will remain alert for these answers to appear over time as we observe people's performances and listen to their dialogs on the world stage, especially those in whom we have a particular interest.

Example Clue Questions to be placed in one's mental repertoire to help gain an overall perspective of a person's dramatic life story in novel form:

If one were to write a novel to describe the story of this person's life, what would be the *story line*?

Throughout this person's life, *what exactly are the values* that he strives to somehow obtain?   What does he desire for life satisfaction?

Examples are found in the preceding listing of *life satisfactions and pleasing activities.*

How does or how will he go about obtaining that which he desires?

Examples of *strategies* for achieving goals are provided in the third session.   Ideas are also provided in Part 4 of these gallery tours.   Key areas of consideration include the acquirement of knowledge and skills.

Where does this person's story begin, where will it go, and where will it end?

Example: Think of the various phases in a person's life, where a person is in each phase, what he is doing, what is happening, and with whom he interacts in each phase. These phases include his childhood, adolescence, early adulthood, middle adulthood, and senior adulthood.

Who are the people with whom this person enacts his life dramas through the various phases of his life?

Examples: family, friends, classmates, career colleagues, business associates, recreational buddies, etc.

What are the *problems* and *obstacles* that he is encountering?

Example: Anything holding him back or standing in the way from achieving his heart's desires.

Can these *problems* and *obstacles* be overcome and if so *how?*

Again, examples of *strategies* for solving problems and overcoming obstacles are provided in the third session. Ideas are also provided in Part 4 of these gallery tours. Key areas of consideration include the acquirement of knowledge and skills.

Once again, the preceding listing of example questions is intended to help establish an *overall perspective* of a person's life story in novel form. As explained earlier, these are questions that we can silently ask ourselves about any person of interest. Typically, the answers will only be revealed over time as we carefully observe and listen to the person. However, if we already know a person fairly well, these answers may then appear rather quickly.

As there are many successive chapters in a novel, there are many successive chapters in a person's life. Normally we see and hear people during their present chapter. Sometimes as we observe and listen to them, they will describe their experiences in earlier chapters. Similarly, they will sometimes share their aspirations for future chapters. A series of example clue questions will now be presented to help us understand the dramas a person is experiencing in the present chapter of his life. These same questions can be easily reworded such that they also apply to past and future chapters, to help obtain a broader understanding of someone's life story.

Example Clue Questions to be placed in one's mental repertoire to help gain a perspective of a specific chapter in a person's dramatic life story:

What in particular does this person desire to obtain in this chapter of his life?

Examples are found in the preceding listing of *life satisfactions and pleasing activities.*

Where, in which *scenes of life*, is this chapter of his life story taking place?

Examples: Home, school, career, social, recreational, etc.

Who are the other *players* in this *scene* with whom this person is enacting this particular drama?

Examples: family, friends, classmates, career colleagues, business associates, recreational buddies, etc.

Are there any particular individuals from *whom* this person desires to receive some form of value? Who are they?

Examples: family, friends, classmates, career colleagues, business associates, recreational buddies, etc.

Does he have certain emotional values to offer that those individuals would appreciate receiving in return from him? If yes, what are they?

Examples: Admiration, Respect, Appreciation, Recognition, Friendship, Love

If not, can he somehow acquire them? How? Which strategies for attainment might he employ?

> Examples are found in the third session. Ideas are also provided in Part 4 of these gallery tours. Generally speaking they are related to acquiring empathic abilities and communication skills.

If an exchange of emotional value has taken place, are both individuals pleased with the outcome, in which case this is a "win-win" situation?

Or, is the outcome instead some variation of "win-lose" or "lose-lose?" *Why?* *What* are the reasons? Can the underlying problems somehow be solved? If so, how?

> Might the answers revolve around the presence or lack of empathic abilities and communication skills, and how they might be developed?

Similarly, if this person is seeking some form of monetary value, which forms of monetary value is he willing to contribute in exchange?

> Example answers: Money, Material Goods, Time and Talent, Career Services

How were these monetary forms of value acquired?

> Examples: Academic study, skill development, career experience, monetary saving, etc.

If he does not have the needed forms of monetary value, can he somehow acquire them? How? Which strategies for attainment might he employ?

This brings us back to the methods for acquiring monetary value as just mentioned.

If an exchange of monetary value has taken place, are both individuals pleased with the outcome, in which case this is a "win-win" situation?

Or, is the outcome instead some variation of "win-lose" or "lose-lose"? *Why? What* are the reasons?

Again as explained previously, the preceding questions are provided as *examples* and are not all-inclusive. Additional questions may come to your mind to also include in your *repertoire* of clue questions.

It is interesting to note the *duration* of various dramas on the world stage. For example, a person might engage in a simple recreational drama that lasts no more than a few minutes or hours. Or, a person may engage in a more complicated drama such as the pursuit of a certain friendship that could take days, weeks, or even months to form. As explained earlier, there can be several phases or chapters in such a dramatic pursuit. Similarly, a person might strive for a certain career position that may entail years of effort to achieve. Here again there could be many dramatic phases or chapters in such a quest.

Example Clue Questions to be placed in one's mental repertoire to help gain an understanding of a person's personality and abilities:

To help avoid extensive repetition, these can be formulated by reviewing the *Principles of Human Nature* presented in the second session.

Example Clue Questions to be placed in one's mental repertoire to help gain an understanding of a person's strategies for attainment:

> Similarly, to help avoid extensive repetition, these can be formulated by reviewing the *Life Strategies* presented in the third session.

Example Clue Questions to be placed in one's mental repertoire to help interpret a person's emotional expressions:

> Again to avoid extensive repetition, these questions can be formulated by reviewing the descriptions of human emotions described in the second session.

Once again as explained previously, the *answers* to these clue questions are to be obtained through careful observation and listening. Much can be surmised from the various players' emotional expressions of satisfaction and dissatisfaction because such expressions are directly indicative of certain values that a person holds dear. If a person is emotionally jubilant about something, the cause of his jubilance is definitely relative to an important value in his life. Similarly, if a person is emotionally distraught about something, the cause of his distress is also relevant to an important life value.

Some people are easier to understand than others simply because they openly discuss whatever is important to them. They tend to freely describe their life dramas verbally in which case all one needs to do is listen. With regard to more quiet private people, one can determine a lot by simply observing their activities, all of which revolve around whatever is meaningful to them.

As one endeavors to be a detective, it is important to note that *all* of a person's activities are value oriented in one way or another. Thus through simple observation one can often *see* the values that his life revolves around, and thereby interpret the associated dramas that he is encountering.

In summary, as you have noticed, all of these clue questions revolve around the fact that every drama in every person's life is associated with the pursuit of value in various forms, mental (usually emotional) or physical (often monetary). All through life each and every person strives for that which he desires. In so doing every person encounters varying degrees of success or failure, pleasure or pain, satisfaction or dissatisfaction—all of which are emotional in nature. With observation and listening skills, along with a repertoire of *clue questions,* over time one can usually detect the underlying motives for the activities in a person's life and the associated emotional dramas.

Tour Guide's Commentary on this Part 3 of our tour:

The intention of this portion of our tour has been to explain the skills of empathy and how they can be developed. While various suggestions for problem solving are offered they are not all-inclusive. Any reader who may be struggling with a serious personal problem is advised to seek professional counseling. For those of modest means, a good person to first contact may be the pastor of one's preferred church affiliation.

We have now completed our tour of the World Chess Game Academy. As you have now witnessed and as was mentioned in the Introduction, in many respects this has been a tour within a tour, or if you prefer—a book within a book. The coursework at this academy has been presented as a preparation for Part 4 of our gallery tours, which soon follows.

Empathic Criticism

Tour Guide's Commentary:

While this World Chess Game Academy is intended to be a primer on the subject of empathy, there are valid criticisms of this academy and its instructional approach that deserve consideration. While it is not possible to foretell every possible criticism, a few of them are anticipated and are addressed in this section.

It may be helpful to begin with a definition of the word "empathy" to help establish a common ground for discussion and criticism. Broadly speaking, empathy is the ability to not only *see* the world from the perspective of another person but to also *feel* the emotions that another person is experiencing. With this broader definition in mind, it may be successfully argued that this academy is *long* on seeing but *short* on feeling. This possible shortcoming is acknowledged in this section.

This writer has made a basic assumption that once a person is able to identify the dramas in another person's life, one will automatically have a sense of the other person's emotional feelings as well. This assumption may be an over expectation. That is because some individuals can clearly see another person's life dramas and dilemmas but at the same time not really care one way or another about the person or what happens to him, and therefore be devoid of feelings for the person.

It may be helpful to clarify the terms "empathy" and "sympathy." To sympathize is to express compassion for another person, particularly for the sorrow he may be experiencing. Sympathy is thus an expression of feeling. To empathize is to identify with and understand another person's life situation and the reasons why he is expe-

255

riencing certain life dramas, whether they be positive or negative. In so doing one may at the same time experience another person's emotions, or maybe not. Here again, some may disagree with this definition and have rightful reasons for doing so.

By likening life to a vast chess game that is being played on a vast worldwide chessboard, there can be a sense of *manipulation.* This is because the basic game of chess is all about manipulating chess people (kings, queens, knights, rooks, and pawns) on a chessboard for the purpose of winning the game. While this can be a useful analogy for describing many events taking place all around our world, there is a certain sense that once the *game of life* is learned, people can then be similarly manipulated to one's personal advantage. This writer's *hope* is that after readers acquire the skills taught at this academy they will form a kind regard for others. With this regard, it is hoped that readers will adopt win-win strategies in their approach to life and their personal pursuits. However, some may argue that this hope is overly optimistic. In summary, it is to be acknowledged that likening the pursuits of life to a skillful game of chess that entails interacting with a multitude of different people has a manipulative connotation. This connotation may seem somewhat *impersonal* and again devoid of feeling. That is contrary to the broader definition of empathy that others may prefer, namely to not only see another person's dramas but to also feel them and be sympathetic.

It is to be noted that the rather unique discussions of empathic reasoning in this text are presented within the context of a broader life philosophy that is also rather unique (as most readers will likely agree). If the importance of empathic reasoning is now understood, this Part 3 will have been a success, whether or not the reader agrees with the definitions and method of instruction.

It is important to acknowledge that there are various alternative explanations of empathic reasoning and its importance by various esteemed authors that deserve consideration. Following in alphabetical order by author's last name are a few of them:

1. *The Power of Empathy—A Practical Guide to Creating Intimacy, Self-Understanding, and Lasting Love*, Arthur P. Ciaramicoli and Katherine Ketcham, Dutton Adult (April 1, 2000), ISBN-10: 0525945113, ISBN-13: 978-0525945116

2. *The Spiritual Power of Empathy—Develop Your Intuitive Gifts for Compassionate Connection*, Cyndi Dale, Liewellyn Publications (October 8, 2014), ISBN-10: 0738737992, ISBN-13: 978-0738737997

3. *Emotional Intelligence—Empathy*, (HBR Emotional Intelligence Series), Harvard Business Review Press (May 9, 2017), ISBN-10: 1633693252, ISBN-13: 978-1633693258

4. *Empathy—What It Is and Why It Matters*, David Howe, Palgrave (December 24, 2012), ISBN-10: 1137276428, ISBN- 13: 978-1137276421

5. *Empathy—Why It Matters, and How to Get It*, Roman Krznaric, TarcherPerigee (November 3, 2015), ISBN-10: 0399171401, ISBN-13: 978-0399171406

6. *The Art of Empathy—a Complete Guide to Life's Most Essential Skill,* Karla McLaren, Sounds True (October 1, 2013), ISBN-10: 1622030613, ISBN-13: 978-1622030613

7. *Finding the Lost Art of Empathy—Connecting Human to Human in a Disconnected World*, Tracy Wilde, Howard Books (May 16, 2017), ISBN-10: 1501156292, ISBN-13: 978-1501156298

An Introduction to Part 4 of these Gallery Tours

Life Mastery

Once again, the purpose of this book is to explain the real purpose for our existence on this planet. This purpose is for all of us to create together as teams to enhance this planet into an ever more beautiful work of art. It has also been explained that through our unique artistic contributions to beautify this planet, we will rightfully receive benefits in return. Namely, we will receive the admiration and respect that we deserve from others in return for our contributions. In many respects, the previous three parts of this book have explained various life principles pertaining to human growth, human understanding, and reasons for our existence. This fourth and last part is primarily focused on applying those principles to make our individual lives true works of art. In this way the title of this book will be fulfilled, namely how to win the respect of others regardless of our race, gender or background.

Life as a Work of Art

Tour Guide's Introduction:

As explained in Part 1 of these gallery tours, the Master Artists had intended this entire world to become a *wondrous work of art*. Rather than directly create this art themselves, they decided to instead embark upon a fascinating artistic experiment. This was to create artists with the ability to create art for them. Human beings thereby became these created artists, and Planet Earth became the chosen location for this artistic experiment to take place.

For these created artists to be truly creative, they were given *free will*. This is because without *free will* they could not possibly be true artists. Instead, they would then be mere illustrators following the directions of other beings that happened to be in charge. With *free will*, human beings are free to create whatever they consider to be artistically beautiful. This includes inner and outer beauty. The Master Artists were hoping for inner beauty in terms of a loving regard of all human beings for each other in the form of harmonious relationships. Their hope for outer beauty was in terms of nature, the environment, healthy plant and animal life, and all the many structures to be created by human beings.

Unfortunately, a certain disease infected a great many of these created artists and the whole world went awry. Anger, fear and suffering became rampant across much of the planet. The disease that caused all of this discord is called SELFISHNESS.

A natural question now arises: What will it take for our world to "get back on track" and into alignment with the Master Artists' original intentions? Possible answers to this question are provided in this Part 4 of our gallery tours. We are now about to consider *how* we might "tune in" to the Inspirations of the Master Artists and strive to make our individual lives masterful works of art, along with the surrounding world in which we live. In so doing, our lives will become true *artistic adventures.*

The Gallery of Friendship and Recognition

Tour Guide's Introduction:

Throughout this entire tour we have been exploring various principles of human nature. In the galleries leading to this one, principles of human empathy were explored. Among the most common situations in which to apply these principles is within the realms of human friendship. To say that each and every person needs a friend and that this is a basic principle of human nature is a statement of the obvious. However, while "friendship" is an everyday term that most of us take for granted, the underlying basis upon which friendships are formed is not always so obvious. Therefore, in addition to understanding principles of empathy, it is helpful to also understand some of the underlying principles of human friendship. These help to explain why we have a natural ability and desire to form a friendship with certain individuals in our lives, but not with others. In this gallery we will explore a few of these principles.

First Word Painting:

In this painting we see two individuals engaged in conversation. They could be two men, two women, or a man and a woman. For the purposes of this painting it does not matter. What we see is that they both have expressions of *personal interest* in the other on their faces, and we wonder what the reasons may be.

(Continued on page 264)

263

(Continued from page 263)

Below this painting is the title, which provides us with a clue: "Personal Friendship." Below this title is a written description of the two individuals depicted there which reads as follows:

"The two individuals seen in this painting are both interested in the subject of their conversation. Each is contributing information. Each is interested in whatever information the other is sharing. We do not know the subject of their discussion. It may be light and impersonal. Or, it may be deep and personal. All we can see is that each is interested in whatever information the other is sharing."

Interpretation:

This painting is basically an introduction to the concept of friendship. When two people can share a common interest and mutually enjoy their discussion of that interest they have the basic ingredients for a friendship. It is to be noted that friendship with another person is an obvious source of mental (emotional) value. However, there is something else in this painting that is not as obvious, but at the same time is of particular interest. This is the *level* of friendship between the two individuals and the *degree* of emotional value attainable at each level. Regarding *levels of friendship* the following clarifications are of interest:[1]

> When two individuals enjoy discussing the *facts* about maybe one or two subjects that are not too personal, they may value each other as occasional casual friends. An example of their discussions might be casual conversations on subjects of gen-

eral interest, such as athletic sports, movies, current news events, etc.

When two individuals enjoy discussing more than just a few subjects but rather a variety of different interests that again are not too personal, they may value each other even more as casual friends, but not close friends. As examples, such individuals may have reasons to meet more frequently because they attend the same school, work for the same employer, or belong to the same organization.

When two individuals are also willing to go beyond obvious facts and discuss their personal ideas and opinions on certain subjects, they are then sharing more of their personal selves. This usually implies a greater depth of friendship and a closer relationship.

When two individuals go so far as to reveal their emotional feelings that are largely personal and confidential, this is an indication that they deeply respect and trust each other. This deeper level of sharing might only be with a few people in a person's life. Such a willingness to share is usually with only the closest of friends.

As stated at the beginning of this section, this painting with its explanation is essentially a clarification of the obvious. It is included here because it is an example of emotional value that all of us cherish. Friendships on all levels are desirable. With some individuals in our lives, casual friendships may be the most appropriate. With others, closer deeper friendships are preferred.

This painting with its obvious subject matter serves another purpose. It provides an introduction to a more important subject that often is not as obvious, that of *personal recognition*. While most will agree that this is a need that every person has, many do not

265

comprehend what is required to offer another person *real recognition*. This realization leads us to the next painting in this series.

Second Word Painting:

In this painting we again see two individuals engaged in conversation. They could again be two men, two women, or a man and a woman. As with the previous painting, it does not matter. What we see is that they both have expressions of *intense personal appreciation* for the other on their faces, and again we wonder what the reasons may be.

Below this painting is its title which provides us with a clue: "Personal Recognition." Below this title is also a written description of the two individuals depicted there which reads as follows:

"These two individuals have both reached a *certain level of competence in a certain field*. At this level of competence they have both experienced a certain degree of success, but may still be striving for additional accomplishments. Reaching their present level of competence was not easy. Significant effort was required. Various obstacles needed to be overcome. Various skills had to be developed to overcome those obstacles. Investments of time and energy had to be made to develop those skills. While their successes may be obvious to many individuals, what it took to reach their level of compe-

(Continued on page 267)

(Continued from page 266)

tence is not. *Only certain cherished individuals have such insight.* The two individuals that we see in this painting recognize the efforts each has made to reach her level of competence. They each understand the obstacles that the other has faced, and the skills that were needed to overcome those obstacles. They understand what it took in terms of time and energy to develop the necessary skills. As a result, the two individuals that we see in this painting are able to award each other due in-depth *recognition* of her life's accomplishments, for which the other is appreciative. This mutual in-depth recognition that they can offer each other is of immense mental (emotional) value to both of them."

Interpretation:

The personal recognition that is described here is the type that all of us desire from at least a few people in our lives. Notice these words in the above explanation: "a certain level of competence in a certain field." The people in this painting could be virtually any two individuals in virtually any life situation. As an example, they could be two students, two athletes, two doctors, two teachers, two farmers, two business people, two construction workers, or two employees in a corporation. Again, they could be any two individuals engaged in virtually any endeavor.

No matter what a person's life situation may be, she has likely encountered certain difficulties that needed to be overcome. While many people do not recognize *what we have been through to get where we are*, whenever that rare person comes along who does so

267

recognize, and can kindly express this recognition, we are appreciative. Again, such recognition from another is of immense mental (emotional) value.

The mutual recognition that we see in this painting is often between two individuals who have traveled along similar pathways, encountered similar obstacles, developed similar skills, and have achieved similar accomplishments. As a result, they are uniquely qualified to recognize what each other has experienced and are able to kindly express this understanding to each other.

For any of us who have even one or two such relationships, we can identify with the emotional value they provide. Personally, each of us has a high regard for those individuals who truly understand us, and are able to kindly express their recognition.

Something else is provided in this painting with its associated explanation. If we truly wish to win the respect and cooperation of another person or group of people, this painting provides us with a *clue* to what is needed: We must develop the ability to recognize their accomplishments and what it took to attain them. The question then becomes: Are we willing to make the effort?

Tribute:

In appreciation for his inspiration and influence upon this writer, here is a brief tribute to John Powell:[1]

★★
★   ★
★   John Powell (1925-2009) was a Jesuit priest and scholar   ★
★   who taught at Loyola University in Chicago. He also   ★
★   became a popular author of many books, some of which   ★
★   ★
★   *(Continued on page 269)*   ★
★   ★
★★★

(Continued from page 268)

became national best sellers. For those who wish to study principles of communication in greater depth, especially one-to-one communication with significant others, you are encouraged to read his book titled: *Why Am I Afraid To Tell You Who I Am.*[1] In this book, he describes five levels of communication in detail, with a warm friendly style that virtually every reader will appreciate.

Also recommended is his companion volume titled: *Why Am I Afraid to Love?*[2] For anyone who is pursuing an enhanced understanding of human relationships and associated issues, his ideas and depth of insight will be appreciated.

Part of the beauty in his writing is that he recognizes the *humanness* in every person. As all of us know, we have strengths as well as weaknesses. No one is perfect. No one! This is important to realize, especially with our closest friends who need our support during the more depressing and embarrassing periods of their lives. The mark of a true friend is someone with whom we can confide our faults and mistakes, and still be accepted. It is important to realize that writers like everyone else have their weaker moments and rightly deserve our compassion and understanding.

Another Tribute:

Also in appreciation for their inspiration and influence upon this writer, here is a brief tribute to both Saundra Hybels and Richard L. Weaver II:

Communicating Effectively,[3] was jointly written by Saundra Hybels and Richard L. Weaver II.

Saundra Hybels (1938-1999) was a teacher of speech communication at Lock Haven University in Pennsylvania. There are now Professor Saundra K. Hybels, Ph.D. Memorial Scholarships issued annually in her honor at that university.

Richard L. Weaver II (1941-   ) is a retired professor of speech communication after having taught more than 80,000 students at Indiana University, the University of Massachusetts, and Bowling Green State University in Ohio where he was nominated for "Best Teacher of the Year."

Communicating Effectively is a college textbook. It is designed to explain the underlying theories of effective interpersonal communication along with how one can develop those skills. Fortunate are the college students who have had the privilege to take communication courses with this text as their guide.

Notes:

1. John Powell, *Why Am I Afraid to Tell You Who I Am?*, Zondervan (May 1, 1999), ISBN-10: 0006281052, ISBN-13: 978-0006281054

2. John Powell, *Why Am I Afraid to Love?: Overcoming Rejection and Indifference*, Thomas More Press (June 1, 1990), ISBN-10: 0883473224, ISBN-13: 978-0883473221

3. Saundra Hybels and Richard L. Weaver II, *Communicating Effectively*, McGraw-Hill Education; 11th edition (March 27, 2014), ISBN-10: 0073523879, ISBN-13: 978-0073523873

The Gallery of Inner Inspirations

Tour Guide's Introduction:

In a few of the previous galleries we were presented with views of how an ideal world might appear. For such views to materialize, people will need to make the most of their lives by growing and blossoming into all that they are capable of becoming. Natural questions then arise: From where will people acquire the *desire* to grow? What will motivate them to invest the necessary time and effort? What will be the source of their Inspiration? How can they open their minds to receive this Inspiration and thereby be filled with the desire to develop their potential and grow into all that they are capable of becoming? Suggested answers in example form are provided in this gallery.

First Word Painting:

In this painting we see a rather simplistic scene. An individual person, man or woman, girl or boy, is comfortably resting alone in a preferred location either indoors or outdoors. Let's assume this person is a woman. Below this painting is a brief essay that describes the nature of her thoughts:

"This person is seeking Internal Guidance by silently asking questions and waiting for answers to appear within the privacy of her mental theater. She realizes that these answers may not always appear immediately,

(Continued on page 274)

273

> *(Continued from page 273)*
> and that some time may be required before a response is received. Never the less, she understands the importance of silently asking key questions and silently contemplating them while waiting for answers to spontaneously appear."

Second Word Painting:

> In this painting we see another rather simplistic scene. It is similar to the previous painting with one difference. Again we see an individual person, woman or man, boy or girl, who is comfortably resting alone, in a preferred location either indoors or outdoors. Let's again assume this is a woman. The only difference we see between this painting and the previous one is that the person is equipped with a writing instrument. This enables her to write down her thoughts as they appear in her mind.

Interpretation:

Many people find it easier to focus their attention on an issue (and not be as susceptible to mental wandering and distractions) when they write down their thoughts as they occur. They therefore engage in a form of silent written dialog. This entails writing down their questions and also pondering them in writing. They then wait for answers to spontaneously appear within the privacy of their minds. Sometimes these answers appear immediately, and sometimes later after a period of time that can extend into hours, days, or longer. When these answers appear, they write them down as well. This process is sometimes referred to as "journaling."

Here is a cautionary note that is somewhat humorous and will cause many tour participants to smile: Since these written thought discourses are personal and private, they are best kept in a private location that is accessible to the writer only. However, there is always a possibility that someday someone will obtain access and read those personal contemplations. It is important therefore to NOT write down one's thoughts on embarrassing issues. Actually, there is no need to. Anything that is troublesome and embarrassing is easy enough to ponder upon, without the need for written description. ☺

Tour Guide's Commentary:

We are curious to know more about the thoughts and questions that the people shown in the preceding two paintings may be pondering and silently asking. Of what significance are they? Suggestions are provided in the three paintings to follow.

Third Word Painting:

In this scene we see a person comfortably seated in a relaxing environment, alone with her thoughts, either with the aid of a writing instrument or without. This person is silently contemplating her present or future role in the body of humanity of which she is a part. As

(Continued on page 276)

(Continued from page 275)

we view the thought screen within her mental theater we see the following thoughts flowing through her mind:

How can I make the most of my life?

What can I contribute to this world that will enable me to experience life satisfaction?

Which are my natural aptitudes, the ones that I was born with?

How can these aptitudes be discovered?

Once discovered, how can they be developed into skills?

Let's consider that I am a single cell in a vast body of humanity. In which systems within this body can my (still to be developed) skills be utilized?

In which systems will I be fairly treated?

Which systems will enable me to receive value in return from others that is equal to what I contribute?

How can I locate a suitable position in one of these systems where I can utilize my skills in a satisfying manner?

How can I maximize the value that I contribute to my body of humanity and thereby maximize the value that I receive in return? Will this be mental (emotional) value, physical (monetary) value, or some combination of both?

(Continued on page 277)

(Continued from page 276)

Could it be possible that enhancing the emotional value in my life is actually more satisfying and important to me?

If I were able to help others grow and maximize the value in their lives, would this be a key source of mental (emotional) value and satisfaction for me?

Which courses of action must I take to obtain the answers to these questions?

Are there any trustful, competent people available who can offer me help and guidance?

How can I find such people to be my advisors?

As this person becomes aware of the two Master Artists and their creative artistic experiment, she conveys the following messages and requests to them:

I know that You can influence and guide my actions but will not conduct them for me. I know that my personal initiative is required.

Please activate my Inner Voice and offer Your Thoughts and Advice!

I realize that if I manage to make my life a true work of art, this is the only value (satisfaction) that You desire in return from me. Please guide me to always offer value to others in return for the value they provide me, either in mental (emotional) or physical (monetary) form.

Fourth Word Painting:

In this scene we see another person comfortably seated in a relaxing environment alone with her thoughts, either with the aid of a writing instrument or without. This person is silently contemplating her relationship with her fellow human beings. As we view the thought screen within her mental theater we see the following thoughts flowing through her mind:

> I realize that every person has an emotional need to receive some form of *recognition* and *admiration* for their positive characteristics from certain people in their life. Recognition and admiration are forms of mental (emotional) value.

> How capable am I when it comes to expressing *sincere* admiration, recognition and appreciation to another person for her positive characteristics?

> I realize that there is a major difference between being *sincere* and *insincere.* One is desirable and the other is not.

> I also realize that people value appropriate recognition and admiration for those inner positive qualities that are NOT very obvious. As an example, to tell a famous movie star that she is a good actor would be an expression of the obvious and fairly meaningless. However, to appropriately express sincere recognition for a certain inner positive qual-

(Continued on page 279)

(Continued from page 278)

ity could be really appreciated by this same famous person, especially if it is one that few others recognize. Needless to say, to obtain the ability to recognize such an inner quality is much easier said than done.

I am coming to realize that to provide appropriate expressions of sincere recognition and admiration to another person for her positive characteristics is a *skill* all in itself.

I am also coming to realize that this particular skill is not always easily developed. If one grows up amongst people who have and practice this skill, one may learn it from them through example. Otherwise, the development of this skill can be a major challenge.

Which of the people that I know would appreciate my sincere recognition and admiration for their positive characteristics?

To which of these people am I capable of expressing sincere recognition and admiration in an appropriate manner?

From which of these people would I appreciate sincere recognition and admiration for my positive traits?

Which of these people have the ability to respond by offering me sincere recognition and admiration?

(Continued on page 280)

(Continued from page 279)

Do I have the ability to recognize the actual positive traits of another?

Do I have the ability to appropriately express admiration to another person?

How can I learn to recognize the inner positive qualities of another person?

How can I learn to appropriately express sincere admiration for them?

How can I learn to form appropriate associations with people with whom mutual exchanges of sincere recognition and admiration are both appropriate and possible?

Are there any people who can offer me help, advice, and training in this area?

How can I find such people?

Who can help me find them?

As this person becomes aware of the two Master Artists and their creative experiment, she conveys the following messages and requests to them:

I know that You can influence and guide my actions but will not conduct them for me. I know that my personal initiative is required.

Please activate my Inner Voice and offer Your Thoughts and Advice!

(Continued on page 281)

(Continued from page 280)

I realize that if I can make my life a true work of art, this is the only value (satisfaction) that You desire in return for helping me.

Please guide me in always offering value to others in return for the value they provide me, either in mental (emotional) or physical (monetary) form.

Fifth Word Painting:

In this scene we see another person comfortably seated in a relaxing environment alone with her thoughts, either with the aid of a writing instrument or without. This person is also silently contemplating her relationship with her fellow human beings. As we view the thought screen in her mental theater, we see the following thoughts flowing through her mind:

I realize that for my expressions of admiration to another person to be meaningful, they must be *sincere*.

To be sincere, they must be truthful. They must be based upon the actual recognition of another person's desirable qualities.

To express sincere admiration for others one needs the *ability* to see the value that they are offering others, privately as well as publicly.

(Continued on page 282)

(Continued from page 281)

This ability begins with the ability to *empathize*. This is the ability to see the world from another person's perspective. This is a skill all in itself. The ability to empathize underlies the ability to recognize another person's positive qualities.

If one is fortunate enough to grow up amongst people who have the ability to empathize, one may learn it from them through example. Otherwise, the development of this skill can be a real challenge.

How can I learn to empathize?

How can I learn to see the world from another person's perspective?

Are there any people who can offer me help, advice and training in this area?

Who can help me find them?

As this person becomes aware of the two Master Artists and their creative experiment, she silently conveys the following messages and requests to them, either with the aid of a writing instrument or without:

I know that You can influence and guide my actions but will not conduct them for me. I know that my personal initiative is required.

Please activate my Inner Voice and offer Your Thoughts and Advice!

(Continued on page 283)

(Continued from page 282)

I realize that if I can make my life a true work of art, this is the only value (satisfaction) that You desire in return for helping me.

Please guide me in always offering value to others in return for the value they provide me, either in emotional or monetary form.

Please offer your guidance in everything I do.

Tour Guide's Commentary:

For any person to make her life a true work of art, she WILL need Inner Inspiration from the Master Artists. The purpose of this gallery has been to provide examples of how such inspiration may be obtained. In addition to the examples provided in this gallery, many other issues will confront a person during the course of her life. They can be dealt with in a similar manner as presented here in this Gallery of Inner Inspiration.

The Gallery of Life Gamesmanship

Tour Guide's Introduction:

The paintings we are about to view in this gallery pertain to the *game of life.* Techniques that people may use to improve their game (enhance their game plan strategies) will be explained. Possibly, as we proceed through this gallery and consider these techniques, we may decide to apply some of them in the *artistic adventures of our lives*—all for the purpose of transforming them into *intriguing works of art.* ☺

First Word Painting:

In this painting we again see our familiar friend Consciousness. Again we see that he is comfortably seated in his mental theater. With some surprise, we see that he is viewing a hand of value cards on his thought screen that life has dealt to him. We then realize that he is contemplating his game plan of life. However, based upon what we can see, we don't know if he knows *how* to play this game effectively or not.

It is to be noted that in this painting we do not see any other players. It focuses solely upon Consciousness and his Mental Theater. As we view the cards that he has been dealt, we see that they are of the following varieties:

Aptitude Cards that can be converted into Skill Cards

Skill Cards that can be exchanged for Physical (Monetary) Value

Skill Cards that can be exchanged for Mental (Emotional) Value

Additional Value Cards that are somewhat mysterious and remain undefined.

Below this painting in bold letters we can read the name of this game that our friend Consciousness is contemplating. This name is *Acquiring Value*. Below this

(Continued on page 287)

(Continued from page 286)
name is a written explanation of how this game is played which reads as follows:

"The object of this game is for Consciousness to enhance his hand of mental (emotional) and physical (monetary) value cards in the best way that he can. Physical (monetary) value cards are desired for the purpose of living in physical comfort. For some, this is a desire for modest surroundings and modest accommodations. For others, this is a desire to live in luxury with considerable wealth. Mental (emotional) value cards are desired for the purpose of experiencing an emotionally pleasing life with love, friendship, and a sense of meaning. For some, this entails having a small group of personal friends. For others, this entails having many acquaintances with extensive interaction. With regard to a sense of meaning, this is associated with personal accomplishments that are beneficial to other individuals, and perhaps to society as a whole.

It is to be noted that Consciousness has a couple of interesting possibilities for self-improvement. One of them is to obtain counseling on how to best improve and play his hand of cards. Another is to improve his hand of cards through investments of time and energy, which are normally in the forms of education and practice. However, it is possible that Consciousness may be unaware of those options, or possibly choose to ignore them if he is."

Interpretation:

Very few people view life as a game of *acquiring value*. Some may even be aghast at this thought. At the same time, whether people realize it or not, they generally live their lives in accord with the rules of this game. What is being described in analogy terms are underlying subconscious thought processes that are inherent in human nature. Most people are not aware of these processes, and certainly most do not interpret them with the use of these same analogy terms. As the word "subconscious" implies, these thought processes operate below one's normal level of awareness. Still, as we observe people's actions on the world stage, we can see that for the most part they DO live their lives in accord with these principles.

The process of acquiring values frequently entails an exchange of values. Typically, one needs to contribute something of value to others in order to receive something of value in return. As explained earlier on these tours, whenever people give something of visible physical (monetary) value or of psychological mental (emotional) value to others, they have a *natural desire* to receive value in exchange that is proportionate to whatever they gave. This is fairly obvious with monetary transactions but less obvious with emotional transactions. One example of an emotional transaction revolves around the *desire* for friendship. If we give someone our friendship we would like to receive their friendship in return or we will be disappointed. This principle also applies to charitable giving where people expect to receive emotional satisfaction in return for their personal generosity. As everyone knows, misunderstandings can easily occur, and therefore the outcome of any exchange may not be what was originally intended or expected. As a result, one or both sides of any value exchange will sooner or later be either satisfied or dissatisfied. In more objective terms, as in a game the outcome of any value exchange can be objectively described as "win-win," "win-lose," or "lose-lose." Also, as in virtually any game of skill, people can enhance their knowledge and skills to thereby become more adept with their value exchanges and achieve more satisfactory winning results. Again, whether people consciously think about these principles or not, subconsciously they live their lives in accordance with them.

The reason why people exchange value with each other is to fulfill natural human desires that can once again be briefly described as follows:

> Every person has a desire to live with some degree of physical comfort.

> Every person has a desire to experience some degree of friendship and love.

> Every person has a desire for personal recognition in one form or another.

> Once a person's basic needs are met, every person desires *something more* in life.

> Generally, people have an inherent desire to *grow* into all that they are capable of becoming. However, this may first become apparent *after* their more basic needs are fulfilled. Once achieved, such an accomplishment and state of mind are of immense personal value.

> Realistically and unfortunately, there are many obstacles in this world that impede the growth of many individuals. On the one hand, deep within every person's subconscious mind is a desire for personal growth, a desire to become all one is capable of becoming, namely to add value to one's life. On the other hand, due to various obstacles that life may present, this desire may never be allowed to grow into being and thereby never materialize.

In spite of all the obstacles, every person has an innate subconscious desire to add value to his life by making it more pleasing and enjoyable in one way or another, in the best way that he can.

As people yearn and strive for *something more* in their lives, they are actually striving to somehow make their lives more beautiful. While they may not consciously view their lives as artistic creations, on a subconscious level they are figuratively striving to transform their lives into pleasing *works of art* (pleasing to them that is, not necessarily to others) through which they can experience personal satisfaction.

As professionally explained in detail by the famous psychologist Abraham Maslow, human life follows an upward pathway of personal growth toward what he termed to be *self-actualization.*[1] At the most basic level people strive to live in physical comfort. Once those basic needs are met, they then seek to fulfill a higher level of personal needs that include the friendship and love of others. Once those needs are met, they then seek to fulfill more complex needs, and so on. This onward and upward *desire* to enhance the value of one's life by fulfilling human needs is an inherent trait of human nature, one that is imbedded in a person's subconscious thought processes. However, the conditions and circumstances of a person's life need to be conducive for such personal growth to occur, or it will not happen. For many people if not most, their personal growth becomes stunted by obstacles they encounter somewhere along their life's journey. In terms of the analogy paintings in this section, overcoming such obstacles entails the use of *skill* in playing one's hand of cards.

Tour Guide's Commentary:

Some may find these ideas difficult to believe, and for understandable reasons. This is because many lives are afflicted with pain—physical and/or emotional. Many live in poverty. Many suffer emotional pain. Many become emotionally injured. Some emotionally injured people preoccupy themselves with desires for revenge. For people who are suffering, their first priority is to somehow alleviate their pain. Physical and emotional distress can dominate people's thoughts to such an extent that there is little time to think of anything else. For them, thoughts of personal growth and life transformation can be very remote, if they even exist at all. For them, their games of value exchanges revolve around their need to alleviate their pain and suffering in whichever ways they can.

Of particular interest are those fortunate individuals who do manage to meet their basic physical (monetary) and mental (emotional) needs, after which they can focus their attention on living more *meaningful* lives. It is these individuals who may then wish to somehow beautify the world around them. While they may not think of their lives in these terms, their desire for personal meaning in life is the basis for various artistic adventures and endeavors that they undertake. They seek meaning through personal contributions that are beneficial to others and society. Some of them strive to help other lives *grow* into beings of greater beauty. Some of these individuals also strive to help society as a whole become more beautiful. Their goals for society may include greater interpersonal harmony amongst its members, as well as enhanced environmental beauty in the surrounding world. It is individuals such as these who we can envy for the impressive value cards that they happen to have. We can also envy them for their expertise in playing those cards. Many of us, this writer included, can only wonder about what it must be like to be in their shoes and to experience their views of the world.

291

For those fortunate individuals who are transforming their lives into adventurous artistic pursuits, we can also wonder about how, when and where they form their amazing ideas and intentions. We might envision them taking time out from the world around them to engage in solitary thought. We might envision them silently contemplating their lives and how they wish to live. It may be during these solitary periods of reflection when they form and refine their life's game plans.

We can also wonder about the sources of their inspirations as they endeavor to transform this world and its societies into true works of art. As we so wonder, we may be reminded of the Master Artists that were introduced to us at the very beginning of these gallery tours. Perhaps, as those gifted individuals strive to transform portions of this planet into magnificent works of art, and as they seek inspiration for this transformation, somehow they manage to *mentally connect* with those Master Artists.

From now until the end of time, the people of this world will wonder about the purpose and meaning of life. What has also just been described is a life philosophy that makes some degree of sense to this writer, but still leaves many questions unanswered. This is the kind of philosophy that *might* be formed after traveling various roads through life. This is not to say that others will form this same philosophy or should. Some may have personal philosophies that are more intricate and refined. Others may have personal philosophies that are more simplistic. Still others might not have any philosophy at all. Maybe it does not matter if people consciously form a life philosophy or not. Regardless of what a person's philosophy of life may be, there will still be questions that will forever remain open ended and always offer new possibilities for intriguing answers.

On a basic level, this writer's suggestion is that every person has a desire to *win* something in life—something of value. This is because people's lives revolve around the pursuit of their personal needs and desires, whether they are consciously aware of this fact or not. These needs and desires can be on either basic or more advanced levels. To obtain them, people normally need the cooperation of others. And normally, this entails giving others something of value to deserve receiving their valuable cooperation in return. Human life tends to be lived in accord with these rules. It is worth mentioning that people do not always win *everything* they desire. Most of us go through life "winning some and losing some." ☺

Second Word Painting:

Here we again have basically the same painting that we have just viewed and interpreted, namely that of Consciousness alone in his Mental Theater contemplating his *game plan* of life. Now, however, we will focus upon a single aspect of this painting, namely that *no other players* are shown.

Interpretation:

It is possible that this Consciousness still has a choice of players with whom to engage in his games and practice his skills (if he has any skills). We can therefore wonder about which players he will choose to be his participants, what value he will choose to contribute to them, and what value he will desire in return. *We can also wonder if his choices will be wise.*

Tribute:

In appreciation for their inspiration and influence upon this writer, here is a brief tribute to both Abraham Maslow and Frank Goble:

According to the online encyclopedia *wikipedia,* Abraham Maslow (1908-1970) is "best known for creating Maslow's hierarchy of needs, a theory of psychological health predicated on fulfilling innate human needs in priority, culminating in self-actualization. He was a psychology professor at Brandeis University, Brooklyn College's New School for Social Research, and Columbia University. He stressed the importance of focusing on the positive qualities in people, as opposed to treating them as a 'bag of symptoms.' A *Review of General Psychology* survey published in 2002, ranked Maslow as the tenth most cited psychologist of the 20th century."

Frank Goble (1917-2000) wrote the book titled *The Third Force: The Psychology of Abraham Maslow,*[1] which clarifies many of Maslow's ideas in layman's terms. Shortly before his death, Abraham Maslow kindly wrote the Introduction to this book, thereby providing his endorsement.

Frank Goble was an aerospace equipment engineer after graduating with a degree in mechanical engineering from the University of California—Berkeley. He became the president of the manufacturing company D.B. Milliken Co. in Arcadia, CA, from which he retired at age 46. He then founded the nonprofit Thomas Jeffer-

(Continued on page 295)

★★

(Continued from page 294)

son Research Center in California to concentrate on developing educational programs to build character. This organization was later renamed the Jefferson Center for Character Education. At the time of this composition, this organization has now evolved into a division of the Passkeys Foundation. Additional information is available at this website: www.passkeys.org/programs/jc_info.html

The ideas described in the previous two paintings have been strongly influenced by Abraham Maslow's hierarchy of human needs theory and his concepts of self-actualization.

★★

Third Word Painting:

In this painting we again return to the *games of life* themes. Here we see an immense building construction site that is still in its initial stages. We see that within this site there will ultimately be a complex of many buildings. A few buildings are shown that are in the beginning phases of construction. For the most part this site consists mainly of vacant space for future buildings that are still in the planning stages, for which construction has not yet begun. Some of the future buildings are not even in the planning stages yet. In front of this site is a sign that reads *"Future Home of the World Mentoring Academy."* On this same sign are additional words that read: *"Applications for voluntary mentoring services are now being accepted. Accomplished seniors regardless of academic credentials are encouraged to apply. Opportunities for abundant mental (emotional) reward await experienced applicants."*

Interpretation:

As we view this painting and ponder its meaning we can reflect back upon a previous gallery that we toured in which the subject of Mentoring was explained. A couple of realizations from that previous gallery again come to mind:

Virtually every person can improve his life experiences (his game of life) with the assistance of a capable mentor for guidance.

While there is an obvious need for virtually every person in the world to have one or more qualified mentors, an actual world-wide system for the provision of such services is still in its initial stages. For the most part, it still remains to be developed.

There is a need for qualified mentors, especially those with life experience.

Senior citizens are valued for their life experience and accomplishments, whether or not they have academic credentials.

Every person desires to receive value in return for services provided. This again is a fundamental trait of human nature, and it applies to mentors as well. Their compensation may be more in the form of mental (emotional) value rather than monetary, especially if they are already established financially. This mental (emotional) value can be derived through the personal satisfaction of helping others and seeing positive results. It can also be derived through social interaction with other like-minded mentors. Within established communities of mentors there would be abundant opportunities for social interaction amongst them.

Tour Guide's Commentary:

Since this proposed *World Mentoring Academy* still remains to be developed, if any person wishes to request the help of a mentor, some effort and ingenuity may be required to find one. A possible source may be any organization of mature individuals with which one has an affiliation. Within such an organization, one can possibly find someone with whom a friendly, informal, advisory relationship can be formed. Through one's voluntary services and contributions to such an organization, one's chances of meeting such an individual and forming a favorable relationship can be enhanced. Here again, the principle of contributing value for the purpose of receiving equal value in return applies.

Another thought comes to mind here: In matters of health care, it is common to obtain second and third opinions. The same principle can apply to mentoring advice. If one feels uneasy with the advice of a certain mentor, it may be wise to seek second and third opinions from other mentors—especially those with differing worldviews.

Fourth Word Painting:

> In this painting we see another vast complex of buildings. Some have already weathered years of time and are still in respectable condition. Others are newly constructed. Others are still under construction. As in the previous painting, there is also vacant space for future buildings that are still in the planning stages. In front of this complex of buildings is also a sign: *"World Education Academy."* On this same sign are additional words that read: *"We offer to increase your value bank of knowledge. Give us your time and energy and we will respond accordingly!"*

Interpretation:

This painting is fairly self-explanatory. Knowledge in a vast variety of fields is readily available. However, investments of time and energy are required for this acquirement.

Selecting a subject of study that entails the use of one's natural aptitudes, and for which there are career opportunities, can be a challenge. Here is where the assistance of a mentoring counselor can be helpful. In addition, taking a formal aptitude test to determine one's natural aptitudes under the guidance of a professional is an excellent recommendation for everyone. The results of such a test can influence one's future direction through life toward new, interesting and rewarding careers.

It is worth mentioning that knowledge can also be acquired through self-study. Books on virtually every subject by insightful authors are readily available. If one happens to be on a tight budget, quality pre-read books are usually available at affordable pricing.

As most are aware, to qualify for many professions, one frequently needs a diploma from an educational institution. As most are also aware, the matter of financing an education can be a challenge. Each and every person's financial situation is unique. Here again, the advice of a mentoring counselor may be needed to help solve financial problems as they arise.

Here is another interesting idea to consider. Self-taught people often have the freedom to form their own independent businesses. While an academic degree may be a requirement to enter a certain profession, such a degree might NOT be required to form an independent business that provides a product or a service to a given industry or profession. As an example, a certain manufacturing company might require certain academic credentials of anyone who wishes to become an employee. At the same time, when considering the purchase of certain products from outside sources, that company's focus will be on the value of the products being offered, and not on the academic credentials of the outside source's ownership. Admittedly, while obtaining a valued academic degree can be a challenge, forming an independent business and achieving success is also a formidable challenge.

Fifth Word Painting:

> In this painting we see another complex of buildings. At the entryway we see another sign: "The World Chess Game Academy." This happens to be the same academy with the four-session curriculum that was described previously.

Interpretation:

It is one thing to have a good hand of value cards, but that is not enough. One is still challenged to find appropriate players with whom to engage in various games of exchange. Once found, persuading them to play can also be a challenge. Once engaged in a game, it becomes a challenge to play one's hand well, especially when seriously in pursuit of win-win results. In essence, in addition to a good hand of value cards, one is also in need of playing skills. Many of them can be developed at the World Chess Game Academy.

Here in this painting we see one of those *best-kept secrets* in this world. In spite of its importance, few people understand the concept of empathy, let along the means for acquirement. It is suggested here that the World Chess Game Academy provides its students a basic foundation of human understanding upon which meaningful communication skills can be developed, and those skills will lead to greater life satisfaction.

Broadly speaking, if one assesses those people who are obviously successful in their field, with a few exceptions they generally exhibit empathic skills. With those skills they have been able to successfully interact with a variety of different people and personalities, and thereby *win* their cooperation.

Tour Guide's Commentary:

As we look around the world stage we see many different people in a variety of situations. Some are enjoying life and others are not. For some, especially those living in poverty, life is not fun and they may be loath to consider it a game.

It is easier to succeed in life if one has the ability to understand one's fellow women and men. Acquiring this ability becomes easier when we begin to recognize that virtually every person strives to improve his life in the best way that he can within the limitations of his beliefs and abilities. This entails adding value to one's life, and as explained previously, such value can be either mental or physical. In this sense, life is like a game, the object of which is to acquire value in various forms. Once we become cognizant of this similarity, people become easier to understand.

With this basic understanding of *life gamesmanship*, the next question becomes that of *how* to apply this understanding. To answer this question, we will proceed to the next gallery on this tour, the *Gallery of Contemplation*, in a search for ideas.

Note:

1. Frank G. Goble and Abraham Maslow, *The Third Force: The Psychology of Abraham Maslow*, (The Introduction is by Abraham Maslow, and the remainder of the book by Frank G. Goble.) Pocket Books (September 3, 1980), ISBN-10: 0671421743, ISBN-13: 978-0671421748

The Gallery of Contemplation

Tour Guide's Introduction:

The previous gallery, like many others along this tour, is filled with unconventional methods of explanation. All of these explanations provide abundant *food for thought* upon which to contemplate. Hence, we will now tour this *Gallery of Contemplation.*

First Word Painting:

In this painting we see another friend in the form of Consciousness seated in her mental theater. We can again see the Thought Screen within this theater, and upon it we see that this Consciousness is also viewing her hand of value cards.

It happens that this Consciousness already has some understanding of the game *Acquiring Value.* The rules of the game have been explained to her and she is now determining how to play her game accordingly. It happens that the person in whom this mental theater resides has a desire to live in some degree of physical comfort and has a desire to enjoy certain luxuries. Therefore, in this painting we see this Consciousness at a moment of time when she is considering the economic realities of life. More specifically, we now see her contemplating a Game Plan for the acquirement of Physical (Monetary) Value.

(Continued on page 304)

(Continued from page 303)

Since this Consciousness is still in the beginning phases of her planning, the stream of thoughts that we see on her screen are mostly in the form of questions as follows:

I know that the specific games for acquiring value that I will find most satisfying are those in which I can utilize my natural aptitudes, whatever they may be.

In which types of careers are my natural aptitudes most needed?

Maybe I have certain aptitude cards that still remain to be discovered. Are there any aptitude testing programs available to help me discover them?

Which are my obvious aptitude cards?

I know that aptitude cards by themselves are not enough. Unless and until they are converted into skill cards they will be of little use.

Which potential skills can I develop, starting with my unique array of aptitude cards?

What will be required to convert my aptitude cards into skill cards? Which forms of training will I need? What will be required in terms of education and practice? What will be required in terms of finance? How can I best finance my training and development?

(Continued on page 305)

(Continued from page 304)

Once they are developed, what will be the best way to play these skill cards to win physical (monetary) value? How much physical (monetary value) will these skill cards actually have? How much will they be worth?

Which players might be interested in the potential skill cards that I might have to offer once they are formed?

With which players will I wish to engage in games of exchange? Which of these players am I apt to like and respect?

Which of these players will treat me fairly?

With which of these players are win-win outcomes possible?

In addition to the acquisition of enough monetary value to support myself, which careers will enable me to experience the personal satisfaction of helping others? In which ways do I truly wish to help others?

Which careers will enable me to make personal contributions to society, in addition to providing enough monetary value to support myself? In which ways do I truly wish to contribute?

Who can help me answer these questions?

(Continued on page 306)

(Continued from page 305)
Are any advisers or counselors available to help me?

Who might be a mentor for me?

Who might be interested in helping me?

How can I find someone to be of help?

Second Word Painting:

In this painting we again see the same Consciousness that we saw in the previous painting, seated in her mental theater. We can again see the Thought Screen within her theater, and upon it we see that this Consciousness is again viewing her hand of value cards.

Once again, we realize that this Consciousness already has some understanding of the game *Acquiring Value.* The rules of the game have been explained to her and she is now determining how to play this game to win. While having given brief consideration to this idea before, she is now more seriously pondering the fact that there is more to life than the mere acquisition of physical (monetary) value. As a result, we now see her contemplating another type of game plan. This Consciousness would like to experience life as an *artistic adven-*

(Continued on page 307)

(Continued from page 306)

ture during which she transforms her life into a true work of art. In this painting we see her contemplating a strategy for this attainment.

As in the previous painting, this Consciousness is still in the beginning phases of her planning. She has some understanding of the game but is largely undecided on how she will play it. On the Thought Screen in this person's mental theater we see her stream of thoughts as she contemplates her future as follows:

> I would like my life to be much more than the simple pursuit of physical (monetary value). I would like it to be worthwhile. I would like to experience *meaning* in my life. I would like to somehow make meaningful contributions. These can be to certain people, to certain institutions within society, or to the world as a whole. How am I to accomplish this?

> As I plan my strategy to engage in a meaningful game of life, I need to be mindful of this basic principle of human nature: People everywhere desire even value exchanges. Whenever they give something of value to others, they expect to receive equal value in return. Otherwise they will feel disappointed. Sometimes they may even feel cheated.

> Coming to terms with reality, I recognize that as a human being I have a desire for personal recogni-

(Continued on page 308)

(Continued from page 307)

tion from others, and this is a form of mental (emotional) value. This is also an innate characteristic of human nature. Every one of us is alike in this way. Every one of us has a desire for admiration, respect, and appreciation from certain people in our lives. How can I live a life in which I can both give and receive such recognition?

I realize that the people to whom I most need to give recognition and from whom I wish to receive due recognition are those individuals who matter most in my life. These include my family, my friends, and those with whom I have educational and career interactions.

I also recognize that whether my personality is reserved or outgoing, either is fine. This is a characteristic that I was possibly born with. Both have their advantages. Both have their place in the world. No matter what my psychological type or archetype happens to be, I know that within me is the potential to make contributions that are both meaningful and valuable. In other words, I know that I have *inherent value*.

I now realize that I would like to share my inherent value with others, and have them share their inherent value with me. I also realize that this can be mentally (emotionally) pleasing for all of us. At this point, I still have these questions:

(Continued on page 309)

(Continued from page 308)

What exactly is my inherent value?

What do I have to offer that might be of interest to others?

What value might I develop that could be of interest to others?

Who are the people that might be interested in what I now have to offer, or will have to offer, whatever that may be?

As I consider these questions, broader body of humanity principles come to mind:

It takes many people to comprise a body of humanity. Within every body of humanity are many systems, and within each system are many people. Each and every person is thereby a cell in a body of humanity.

Every person has growth potential.

Every person has the potential to fill a meaningful position somewhere within a body of humanity. Once found, this is a position in which a person can contribute meaningful value to the body and receive life-sustaining value from the body in return.

Some people have found such a meaningful cellular position and are actively fulfilling it.

(Continued on page 310)

(Continued from page 309)

Some people have NOT yet found such a position. At the same time they are pursing one as a goal and are making significant progress toward its attainment.

Some people have NOT yet found such a position and for various reasons are not pursuing one. They of course need advice, encouragement, and guidance.

Again, the cellular positions that people find most satisfying are those in which they can utilize their natural aptitudes.

And again, no cellular position anywhere in the body of humanity can be emotionally satisfying unless that person is receiving equal value from the body in proportion to what she contributes.

As I formulate this game plan and consider various principles of human nature and communication, certain realizations dawn in my mind:

What if I had the ability to recognize a person's position in the body of humanity along with the value she is contributing? What if I also had the ability to provide additional value that would enable a person to be even more effective in her position? Such ability on my part would be sincerely appreciated.

(Continued on page 311)

(Continued from page 310)

Similarly, what if I had the ability to recognize a person's pathway toward a certain position in the body of humanity and the progress she has made? What if I also had the ability to provide additional value that would enable the person to make additional progress along her pathway? Such ability on my part would also be sincerely appreciated.

Also, what if I had the ability to recognize a person's lack of progress toward a meaningful position, along with the associated reasons? What if I also had the ability to help a person resolve certain problems and thereby make meaningful advancements? Here as well, such ability on my part would be sincerely appreciated.

In summary, what if I had the ability to help others grow as individuals in one way or another and thereby help them advance along their pathways through life? This would be a meaningful value contribution. Such ability on my part would be sincerely appreciated.

I can now see that I may need a greater understanding of various systems within society in order to offer others due recognition and appreciation. Possibly I need to acquire more knowledge in certain areas—possibly a lot more knowledge. Thankfully, reading materials are readily available and affordable.

(Continued on page 312)

(Continued from page 311)

I can also see that to give people the sincere recognition that they desire and deserve, I may need to develop additional communication skills.

Now, as I again view and evaluate my hand of emotional value cards, I am forming these conclusions along with a strategy for playing them:

Some of these are knowledge cards. They represent knowledge that I already have about human society, certain systems or institutions within society, and certain people within these systems or institutions.

I have an interest in acquiring additional knowledge cards regarding certain subjects that are of interest to me. My reasons may be for personal enjoyment, or because I can see that certain knowledge cards will help me advance toward my goals.

I also have an interest in acquiring additional knowledge cards pertaining to subjects that are of interest to others. This knowledge will provide me with a common ground for conversation with them. A simple principle of human nature is that people with similar interests enjoy discussions with each other. This becomes especially true when these discussions are intellectually stimulating.

Some of these cards in my hand are skill cards. They represent the skills of human interaction that I already have. I would like to acquire additional

(Continued on page 313)

(Continued from page 312)

communication skill cards. My reasons include a desire to more effectively interact with all the people in my life—personally and professionally. I would like additional conversational skill cards that will help me engage in meaningful discussions. I would also like additional empathy skill cards that will help me relate with others more easily.

As I view my potential hand of emotional value cards, including those that I already have and those that I still plan to acquire, I am also viewing the people in my life. With which of them do I wish to engage in games of value exchange? What will I have to offer that will be of value and of interest to them? What will they have to offer that will be of value and of interest to me?

Similarly, I am also considering certain people or certain types of people that could be in my life, once my hand of cards is more fully developed. Again, with which of them will I wish to engage in games of value exchange? What will I have to offer that will be of value to them? What will they have to offer that will be of interest to me?

How can I improve this hand of cards? Who can help me? Where can I go to find help? Who might be my advisors or mentors?

Third Word Painting:

In this painting we see another Consciousness within the mental theater of another person. Again we have a view of her thought screen. It happens that this Consciousness would also like a sense of *meaning* in her life. She would like her life to be worthwhile. She would like to make meaningful, valuable contributions that are beneficial to others. We therefore see the following stream of thoughts and ideas on her thought screen:

Thinking of my family, what can I offer them that will enrich their lives? What specifically do they need? How can I help them grow and advance along their pathways through life? What kinds of appropriate help, advice, encouragement, recognition, etc. might I offer them? What would be an appropriate way in which to do this?

Thinking of my friends, what can I offer them that will enrich their lives? What specifically do they need? How can I help them grow and advance along their pathways through life? What kinds of appropriate help, advice, encouragement, recognition, etc. might I offer them? What would be an appropriate way in which to do this?

Thinking of the social organizations to which I belong, is there something of value that I can offer

(Continued on page 315)

(Continued from page 314)

them? What specifically do they need? What would be an appropriate form of participation or involvement for me?

Thinking of my career associates, what kinds of contributions can I make to their lives? What specifically do they need? What would be appropriate? What would be an appropriate way in which to make those contributions?

Fourth Word Painting:

This painting is similar to the previous one. On a somewhat grander scale, it depicts a particular Consciousness and mental theater that *might* represent the minds of certain people *in positions of power and influence*. On the thought screen within this theater we can see the questions that such a Consciousness *might* consider. These same questions may also appear within the minds of those who *aspire to positions* of power and influence. The stream of possible thoughts that one *might* observe on the thought screen in such a theater include:

What about the body of humanity in which I am a part?

(Continued on page 316)

(Continued from page 315)

More specifically, what about the economic system within this body in which I am a career participant?

What might I contribute to improve this system?

Can I in some way improve this system's performance?

Is there anything I can do to help it function more harmoniously or more efficiently?

Is there anything I can do to help this system better meet the needs of society?

Fifth Word Painting:

This painting is similar to the previous two. On an even grander scale, it depicts a particular Consciousness and mental theater that *might* represent the minds of certain individuals who have been of historical significance. On the thought screen within this theater we can see a stream of thought questions that such a Consciousness *might* have considered. These include:

What can I do to improve the world as a whole?

What can I do to improve world society?

(Continued on page 317)

(Continued from page 316)

Which new and additional systems can I introduce to the world that will prove to be beneficial?

What will it take to establish these systems?

What will be the best approach?

Which individuals might be of assistance and willing to participate in this all new venture?

How do we get started?

Tour Guide's Commentary:

As we view the various paintings in this gallery and consider the fact that the Consciousness depicted in them is silently asking questions and considering various possible answers, a few questions may dawn in our minds:

Might this Consciousness be directing any of her questions to the Master Artists for their advice?

What might be the answers she is likely to receive from these Master Artists?

Will she take their advice seriously?

Will she have the courage to follow through and implement their suggestions?

The Gallery of Higher Consciousness

Tour Guide's Introduction:

This next series of paintings is a departure from those in the previous gallery in that they provide a series of examples that are admittedly somewhat light-hearted and less serious views of what *might* be described as forms of *higher consciousness.* Yes, there will be reasons to smile. ☺

First Word Painting:

> Here we see a passenger comfortably seated in an airplane looking downward at the landscape below. This passenger happens to be observing an automobile traveling along a roadway. Thanks to his elevated view from the airplane, this passenger is able to see a great distance of the road behind the car and a great distance of the road ahead. In other words, this passenger can see not only where the car is, but also where it has traveled from, and where it is about to travel. From his elevated vantage point in the plane, this passenger can see *more* of the road ahead than the driver of that car can. Maybe the driver of the car knows the road ahead, and maybe he does not. Either way, the passenger in the airplane overhead does, thanks to his elevated position and the expanded view that he thereby has.

319

Second Word Painting:

In this painting we see a certain Consciousness comfortably seated in his mental theater. We can also see that, of the two screens in his mental theater, his focus is on the external world screen. We can see that screen and upon it we can see that his focus is on a single individual. He can see where that person is in life, where that person has been in life, and where that person is headed in life. Maybe the person being observed has a clear view of his life ahead, or maybe he does not. Either way, the Consciousness in this mental theater does.

It is also to be noted that within this particular mental theater a certain diploma is on display that indicates this person is a graduate of (you guessed it) the World Chess Game Academy! ☺

Interpretation:

We can easily see the correlation between the Consciousness in this particular theater and the passenger in the airplane that we saw in the previous painting. We can also easily see how these two paintings help to clarify the concept of advanced awareness or higher consciousness.

In addition, we see the credit given to the World Chess Game Academy. An underlying suggestion provided in this painting is that the pathway to higher consciousness *can* pass through this academy.

Third Word Painting:

This painting depicts another Consciousness seated in his mental theater. This might be the Consciousness of a person who is accomplished in his particular career, possibly in the world of business or government, or possibly in another profession.

This particular Consciousness has already made significant progress in both planning and implementing his life game plan. On his thought screen we see that he is evaluating his hand of value cards—mental (emotional) and physical (monetary). On the other screen in his theater, the one that views the external world, we see that he is observing and evaluating various players on the world chessboard.

As we observe the external worldview of this Consciousness, we see that he has the unique ability to perceive the physical (monetary) and mental (emotional) value cards in other players' hands. In addition, he can perceive how those individuals are playing their cards. He can perceive what they are striving to win, and he can perceive the strategies that they are employing to win.

We also see a display wall within this theater. On this wall is also the diploma from the World Chess Game Academy, indicating that he has attended there and graduated. As we again observe the thought screen

(Continued on page 322)

> *(Continued from page 321)*
>
> within his mental theater, we can see that he has also developed the ability to recreate and observe the dramas of other people's lives on this screen.

Interpretation:

In essence, what we see in this painting is a Consciousness that has made significant investments of time and energy to enhance his hand of cards along with his skill in playing them.

We can be impressed with his ability to recreate and observe the dramas of other people's lives on the thought screen within his theater. He is able to perceive what other players are specifically striving to achieve in life. He is also able to perceive what it is that certain people really value, what their strategies are for attainment, and how well they are succeeding.

As this Consciousness views various players on the world stage and decides how best to implement his personal game plans, whatever they may be, he is able to make these observations:

He can *perceive* which players have value that he desires.

He can *perceive* which players have a need for value that he can offer them in exchange.

He can *perceive* which players have an actual interest in making such an exchange.

Based upon these perceptions, he can easily *determine* the best approach for negotiating appropriate exchanges of value.

Fourth Word Painting:

This painting is somewhat similar to the previous one. We see another close-up view of a Consciousness within the mental theater of a person. This might also be the Consciousness of an accomplished professional, possibly in a field of business, government, education, philosophical inquiry, or virtually any other profession. This Consciousness has skills similar to those explained in the previous painting, but with additional refinements.

This Consciousness has also graduated from the World Chess Game Academy. In Shakespearean terms, he has developed a unique view of the world stage. Some will find this view to be intriguing. Others may be a little wary, realizing that such an individual could be rather manipulative if he chose to be. While this is not the same view that every academy graduate acquires, it is nevertheless an interesting view and worth our time to consider.

On the outer worldview screen in this mental theater we can see that this Consciousness sees the world stage as an elaborate chessboard. In this view, every person is seen as a player on this board. The life of every person is viewed as a sequence of dramatic occurrences as he attempts to move from Point A to Point B. In addition, Point A is perceived to be one position within a body of humanity and Point B is perceived to be another more desirable position within a body of humanity—a posi-

(Continued on page 324)

(Continued from page 323)

tion with more value potential—either monetary, emotional, or both.

As in a conventional game of chess, every player on the board is perceived to have certain moves available to him. In other words, every player has the opportunity to move in certain directions to certain positions, but is denied the opportunity to move in other directions to other positions. Therefore, as with a conventional game of chess, those players with greater movement capabilities have access to more positions, some of which offer greater opportunity.

Furthermore, every player's ability to move about on the world chessboard and fill certain positions is determined by the value cards in his hand, and his skill with playing them. Those who somehow manage to enhance their hand of value cards and improve their playing skills can thereby advance to more desirable positions.

This same Consciousness perceives the world chessboard as being fairly easy to navigate for those who are rich with emotional value cards and who have skill with playing them. While monetary value cards are important, they are considered less significant. This is because those who are rich with emotional value typically are able to apply those skills to acquire enough monetary value to live comfortably, either in humble or more luxurious surroundings—whichever they prefer.

Interpretation:

This painting provides us with a unique perspective of the world as interpreted by a well-developed Consciousness that resides within the mental theaters of certain people. Again, this is not necessarily the same view that the Consciousness of every well-developed person has. Many interpret life and the world differently. Still, this is an interesting perspective, and if we use this perspective to view various players on the world chessboard we can make some interesting observations:

Different people play their individual games of life differently.

Some players have a Point B in mind and a plan to reach it, while others do not.

For those who have a plan, some plans are feasible and some are not.

Some players select a Point B that is fairly easy to attain. Others select a Point B that is challenging and difficult to attain.

Some players give due consideration to a certain Point B, and decide it is not worth their time or effort to attain. Instead, they choose an easier, less challenging position as their goal.

For some, there are a number of intermediate points between A and B, and they formulate separate game plans for advancement to each intermediate point in succession.

For some, the experience acquired at each point is a prerequisite for advancement to the next point.

For some, their plans for advancement from point to point across the board entail the acquirement of additional knowledge and skills in each successive position. This may be acquired formally through educational institutions or informally through self-study and job experience.

For some players, their satisfaction in life is the journey toward Point B, not in the actual attainment. They therefore set their goals high and are satisfied with whatever progress they make. They never expect to actually reach Point B. Instead, they simply proceed in that general direction, and again are satisfied with whatever progress they make.

Many people, especially those in retirement, have already progressed as far as they intend to on the world chessboard. They are content with their present hand of value cards. For them, their game plan may be to simply retain the position that they have already attained and hold on to the cards that they already have.

Tour Guide's Commentary:

This next painting is essentially a duplicate of one that we studied earlier in the Second Session of the World Chess Game Academy. It is inserted here again because it serves to further clarify the concept of *higher consciousness.*

Fifth Word Painting:

In this painting we again see our friends Consciousness and Sub-consciousness busily creating audio-visual presentations of people's life dramas for private viewing within their mental theatre.

Interpretation:

As Consciousness and Sub-consciousness create these audio-visual presentations they are endeavoring to *empathize* with people, namely to see and understand the lives of others from the perspective of those others. The degree to which one can empathize with other individuals is an indication of one's level of consciousness. **As one learns to empathize with more and more people and as one learns to understand increasingly complex facets of people's lives, one's level of consciousness rises accordingly.** To help explain this in more detail, consider the many different aspects of life:

Consider the bodies of humanity and the cells within these bodies, each of which is an actual human being.

Consider the many systems within these bodies, examples of which include: family, social, recreational, educational, philosophical, economic, governmental, etc. All of these systems have something in common in that they are designed to provide some combination of mental and emotional value to the people they serve.

Consider the many different positions that people occupy within these systems.

Consider the various levels of responsibility within these systems.

Consider the many different types of value exchanges that take place between individuals within these systems.

Consider the many different individuals aspiring to various positions within these systems.

Consider the many different motivations and goal plans that people have to advance within these systems and become situated in desirable positions. Consider the challenges they face, and the obstacles they encounter.

Consider the many different emotional experiences that people encounter across the broad spectrum of human emotions, from extreme pleasure to extreme pain.

The more one is able to empathize with individuals and the many complexities they face in all aspects of their lives in our broad diversity of world situations, the higher will be one's level of consciousness. Another way of saying this is that the higher one's level of consciousness happens to be, the greater will be one's understanding of the many *varied and diverse dramas* of human life taking place all around this planet amongst all groups of people and at all levels of society.

A conclusion one may therefore draw is that for some individuals a first step toward advancement in consciousness can be careful study at the World Chess Game Academy.

Sixth Word Painting:

In this painting we have another view of the thought screen within a mental theater in which there is a Consciousness that is gifted with a clear view of the world chessboard.

On this thought screen we can see an *ideal view* of the world that this Consciousness would like to see. He plays his game of life to make advancements toward this ideal view. However, he realizes that before this view can actually be seen many changes will first need to be made all across the world chessboard. Because of the immense difficulties involved, and with a realistic assessment of the time required for attainment, this Consciousness knows that he will never actually see this view actualized during his lifetime, but will still extend his best efforts for attainment anyway. For him, the experience of simply making progress toward the achievement of this ideal view is in itself a source of personal satisfaction.

This ideal view that this Consciousness would like to see is one in which the entire world has become a true work of art. Such a view includes the following world accomplishments:

Each and every person's natural aptitudes are discovered.

(Continued on page 330)

(Continued from page 329)

Each and every person has the opportunity to develop his natural aptitudes into skills.

Each and every person has the opportunity to utilize his natural aptitudes in his career, whatever it may be.

Each and every person is also fulfilling his natural archetypal role on the world stage.

Each and every person has the opportunity to utilize his skills to contribute maximum value to the world.

Each and every person is able to receive equally as much value in return from the world as he contributes to the world.

Personal Guidance Systems are in place to make the preceding ideals possible, especially with the aid of mature mentors.

There is universal recognition that personal problems often stem from childhood abuse and neglect. There is a universal understanding that the minds of world tyrants were often formed through the pains they endured during childhood. Therefore, there is a universal effort to prevent such abuse and neglect, and thereby help every child and adolescent get off to a good start in life. As a result, each and every person has access to qualified mentors for guidance from early childhood onward.

(Continued on page 331)

(Continued from page 330)

Each and every person has the ability to access an Inner Source for inspiration and guidance.

There is a universal desire for environmental health and beauty everywhere.

Both plant and animal life are carefully managed to enhance their natural beauty all around the world.

Extensive effort is made to alleviate animal suffering everywhere, including that of farm animal suffering. This in itself becomes an art form.

The above attainments offer extensive mental (emotional) value to people everywhere. As a result, the attainment of mental (emotional) value takes precedence over monetary value. At the same time, every person is rewarded with enough monetary value to live comfortably. Realizing that there is a limited availability of material resources on this planet, excessive luxuries are not considered important. On the other hand, universal mental (emotional) satisfaction IS considered extremely important.

In a world as described in this painting, people everywhere interact with each other in such a way as to comprise larger bodies of humanity that are dedicated to creating beautiful works of art the world over, both externally and internally. Each and every person is comforted, guided, and motivated through *Inner Inspiration.*

Tour Guide's Commentary:

A Consciousness that is gifted with a clear view of the world can have a desire for this world to become a true work of art. He may have an idealistic view of what this world could someday become. He may realize that this view is not attainable during his lifetime. At the same time, he may believe that some degree of progress toward this idealistic view is possible. Therefore, any progress that he is able to make becomes a source of personal satisfaction.

A Consciousness with this perspective of the world is likely to adopt a "win-win" strategy. He will recognize that the key to his advancements on the world chessboard is to help others in their quests for advancements. Simply stated, he offers contributions that help others advance in exchange for their contributions to help him advance.

With this perspective, such a Consciousness is motivated to pursue a world situation in which every person is able to fully develop his potential and experience life satisfaction. In such a world people could harmoniously interact to comprise larger bodies of humanity. These larger bodies of humanity could function as artists dedicated to creating beauty everywhere around the world, both in the external physical realms, and in the internal realms of every person's mentality.

In the view of such a human Consciousness, a live vibrant world of interacting accomplished individuals would indeed be beautiful—a true work of art. Every person's life would thus be an *artistic adventure* of growth, development, accomplishment, and satisfaction. **That of course is what our Good Friends, the Master Artists, had in mind all along.**

Cheers! ☺

About the Author

As a reader you deserve some understanding of the writer. Since this text is largely devoted to the subject of human understanding, it is only fair to provide you with some understanding of the person that produced this manuscript. Since this book is likely to long outlive me, and since I am not likely to make many public appearances, this section is intended to offer a few insights. As you are about to read, it is somewhat of an autobiography.

As you review my background you will NOT find any academic credentials in areas of psychology or philosophy. Virtually everything that I have learned throughout the seventy-plus years of my life that is being shared with you in this text has been acquired through life experience and informal education. However, I hasten to add that I have learned much from the writings of various distinguished individuals that have had extensive academic training. Throughout this text they are given due credit for the influence they have had on my life.

For me, it is always interesting to know a little about a person's ancestral background. Mine differs from many if not most writers in this field. As near as I can tell, from my parents all the way back, all of my ancestors were farmers, presumably for hundreds of generations. I like to think of them in more eloquent terms as "practitioners of plant and animal husbandry." ☺ I am a third, fourth, and fifth generation descendent of immigrants from Germany and Austria. All of them arrived during the 1800's, and all of them homesteaded farmland in the State of Minnesota. I believe that all of them originated in the rural peasant classes of northern Europe.

As for myself, I grew up on a farm until the age of ten. My parents then moved to the city of New Ulm, Minnesota, a small town of around 15,000 inhabitants located in the south central part of the state. Had that move not taken place, for better or worse I might never have left the farm and evolved into a city dweller.

For me, it is also interesting to know how a writer acquired certain interests. My fascination with the principles of human nature began during my early childhood years. My situation was unique in that out of the seven children in my father's family, only three married and I became the only grandchild. In addition to my parents, I dearly loved my uncles and aunts. They were kind hearted and treated me well. I was a bright spot in their lives and a source of happiness for them. Through them, their kindheartedness, their rural roots, and their love for nature and animals, I also acquired a fondness for the scenic beauty of nature and a heartfelt concern for animals. At the same time, they were a dysfunctional family in that it was hard for them to fit in with the rest of our community. They had good intentions but lacked the ability to relate with others outside their immediate family. In contrast to their situation, there were nine children in my mother's family from which fifty-five of us first cousins emerged. With the usual "ups and downs" that most families encounter, they were normal healthy people who kindly accepted me "as one of them." Similarly, my classmates throughout my school years (again with typical "ups and downs") were for the most part normal healthy individuals from normal healthy families. As a result, from early childhood onward, I wondered why there was such a contrast between my father's family and the other people in my life. After many years I came to the conclusion that their lives would have been far more pleasant if they would simply have had more *empathic* abilities. I believe they would then have had a broader circle of friends, and would have been able to better fit in with the others in our rural community.

Admittedly, during my earlier years I also suffered with a lack of empathic ability. I had many problems. That has added to my motivation to better understand others, especially those with well-developed personalities. My ambition has been to somehow discover their secrets and apply them to my life, hoping to further develop my own personality as a result. This remains a continuing ambition, since I have discovered that there is always more to learn, and always room for improvement.

Upon completing secondary school at Cathedral High in New Ulm, I made a decision to attend college. This was with the strong encouragement of the teachers at Cathedral, many of whom were dedicated nuns and priests, to whom I remain grateful for their inspiration and guidance. I am also grateful for the friendship of my classmates throughout those twelve years of primary and secondary school who somehow accepted and endured my idiosyncrasies. ☺

My selection of a major in college was based upon my interests at that time. Throughout my school years I had spent summers doing farm work for relatives and in so doing learned to operate farm machinery. In this way I became somewhat mechanically inclined. Throughout my years in high school, the mathematics and science courses had a special appeal to me. Mechanical Engineering therefore became a logical choice for a college major. Somehow, the Milwaukee School of Engineering in Milwaukee, Wisconsin entered my "dreams for the future," which I then attended. This turned out to be a very "no-nonsense" engineering school that provided an excellent preparation for a career in the manufacturing industries.

An issue in most young men's lives is that of military service. For anyone who may be interested, after my college graduation in 1968 the United States Army classified me as "4-F", resulting in a physical deferment from service due to both a spinal curvature and high blood pressure caused by a partially obstructed renal artery. Otherwise I might have been called to serve in Vietnam, and might not have survived.

I then began my engineering career in Minneapolis, Minnesota. However, the matter of finding a satisfying position in the American industrial world became more difficult than I had anticipated. After considerable frustration in unsatisfying career positions, I encountered a kind adviser who referred me to a professional psychologist. This psychologist happened to be a senior gentleman with a lifetime of experience. He has now passed away and I look back at him as having been a psychological genius. He administered a battery of tests – aptitude, vocational interest, and personality. Based upon those test results he prepared a written analysis that absolutely amazed me. I discovered that once armed with those test results he knew me better than I knew myself. His final conclusions and recommendations essentially were: "*Persuasion* is a mode of thought that appeals to you. You still need to develop additional people skills, but a sales career would interest you. With your engineering background, a career in technical sales is a logical course of action." Those recommendations surprised me somewhat because I am a rather reserved person, and hardly fit the stereotypical image of a salesman with an extraverted personality. Still, I followed that advice and found that he was right. I had many people skills that still needed to be developed (and are still in a stage of development). I did pursue a career in technical sales in the industrial world, and it has been an interesting way to earn a living. It has also been a life-long adventurous emotional roller coaster ride with many ups and downs in the form of sales wins and losses. In addition, it has been a career rich with learning experiences during which I have met a multitude of different people from a variety of different backgrounds. As a matter of interest, this same psychologist suggested that I am the type who may someday be motivated to make a contribution in the field of human understanding. At the time, I took that suggestion with a proverbial *grain of salt,* not really believing him. To my later surprise, I began to fulfill that prophecy with the preparation of this manuscript. Without a doubt, my counseling sessions with that psychologist marked a major turning point in my career and life.

Upon my entry into the world of technical sales at the age of 25, the development of additional people skills became paramount. I wanted to understand people as well as I understood engineering. I thus developed an all-consuming fascination with psychology. This has become and remains a life-long interest. I have attended various seminars and reviewed numerous books on the subject. The library that I have accumulated over the years now numbers in the hundreds. Along with this interest in psychology is a curiosity about the reasons for our human existence, and why we are as we are. This, of course, is the trait of a philosopher.

Some readers may be inclined toward conventional psychological analysis. For those who are curious to analyze this writer, I don't mind volunteering what may be considered *basic information*: Personally, I have been deeply interested in the principles of psychological types that originate with the famous Swiss psychologist Carl Jung. Those principles have been expanded upon by Isabelle Briggs Meyers in her book *Gifts Differing,*[1] by David Keirsey and Marilyn Bates in their books titled *Please Understand Me*[2] and *Please Understand Me II,*[3] and by various other authors. The Meyers Briggs Type Inventory test is fairly well known at the time of this composition. My type is that of an INXJ, which is on a scale midway between INTJ and INFJ. As it happens, many engineers are INTJ's. As it also happens, many writers are INFJ's. For anyone who is interested, I will digress a little here: As explained by

Isabelle Briggs Meyers, all the types are associated with unique gifts, gifts that differ from type to type. In addition, every person can and should be proud of his or her type, whatever it happens to be. All of them are good and desirable in their own way. As far as I am concerned, those particular books on psychological type should be *must reading* for virtually everyone.

Another of the best books I have read that will help explain my personality is titled *About Men and Women*[4] by Tad Guzie and Noreen Monroe Guzie, a husband and wife team. It revolves around the concept of Archetypes. I believe this concept also originates with Carl Jung. Through the genius of Tad and Noreen, this concept has been expanded upon in a manner that is easy to understand, and entertaining besides. They describe four male archetypes of *Father, Warrior, Seeker, and Sage,* and four corresponding female archetypes of *Mother, Amazon, Companion, and Mediatrix.* Through this book I discovered that my personal archetype is on a scale between that of *Seeker* and *Sage.* The *Seeker* within me helps account for my lifelong search for human understanding. The *Sage* in me has formed what I believe to be a rather unique philosophical outlook on life and the world. As I awakened to the hard economic facts of life, namely that one needs to somehow earn a living, the *Seeker* in me discovered that *seeking* tangible industrial equipment business as a sales person is a practical occupation for an engineer, and a satisfying one. At the same time, my *search* for human understanding has always had a higher priority. Once again, *About Men and Women* with its wealth of fascinating insights has answered many questions for me. On a more professional level, and in a separate section, this same book provides a clarification of how Archetypes differ from Psychological Types. This is a clarification that may be of interest to many psychologists. Virtually every person regardless of background or philosophical persuasion would find this book to be both beneficial and enjoyable. In my view, it is one of this world's *best-kept secrets.*

Here is another brief digression: While discussing the subject of largely unknown authors, I will mention another that has had a significant influence upon my thinking. Brian P. Hall has written various books with such titles as *The Development of Consciousness,*[5] *Developing Human Values,*[6] *Values Shift,*[7] and *The Genesis Effect.*[8] Those books are far more academic and sophisticated than this one, and are likely to have particular appeal within academic communities. To help explain what I mean I will suggest that we first reflect back upon human history and think of certain individuals who are famous for their profound understanding of life. These are the individuals who began major movements of thought, whose contributions influenced many succeeding generations, and whose teachings have become central points in many people's lives. As we think of them we can better understand a popular philosophy of life, namely that we are all on a journey from lower to higher consciousness. As for myself, if I ever manage to reach a halfway point on this journey I will consider myself lucky. The fact remains that many readers of this book will have already progressed farther along this upward pathway to higher consciousness than I can ever hope to. While such individuals may be in search of answers that are not found in this text, they are likely to discover important insights in Brian P. Hall's writing. He explains the upward pathway to broader consciousness in fascinating detail. His books are well researched and are written on a professional level. Many, especially those in the academic and professional realms, will appreciate his contributions. In addition, he has the academic credentials that many readers value in an author. As for myself, I feel fortunate to have discovered his work.

The preparation of this manuscript began in January of 1981 with a creative writing course at Minnesota State University in Mankato, Minnesota (the one and only course I ever enrolled in there). It has now taken some forty years for completion. Much of this time has been invested in a research phase with a struggle to make sense of our differing human mentalities and the extremely complex world in which we live. The severe inequalities, tragedies, and injustices that have occurred and continue to occur have always been of deep concern to me. Repeatedly I have wondered about the reasons for so much injustice and unfairness. Finding a means of expression that *ordinary people on the street like me* might find appealing and hopefully entertaining has also been a major challenge. Since I do not have formal academic credentials in psychology or philosophy, I knew that my book would need to be written in *novelty form* for it to catch on. The idea of composing this in the form of an art gallery tour has served me well, and first occurred to me during the last few years of preparation. By that time, I had retired from my life-long engineering career and had more time available for personal writing. As you have witnessed throughout this text, I have a liking for analogies and love to use them in my explanations. Possibly, this comes with training as an engineer, which is largely visual in nature. For those who are unaware, virtually every concept in engineering school is explained with the aid of a visual diagram. That explanatory approach has now carried over into this manuscript in which I explain many concepts with the aid of word pictures. What may also be possible is that a life that has been filled with unconventional experiences has left me ill equipped to write a conventional text. ☺

Another more lighthearted question about me may also come to a reader's mind, this one concerning the subject of female companionship. I will answer this question somewhat *"tongue in cheek."*

Throughout my life I have been attracted to beautiful women, and this has sometimes lead to rather unrealistic pursuits. To my chagrin, they have often found me to be an easy person to manipulate. ☺ Also, my emotional roller coaster career in sales and my preoccupation with psychological-philosophical searching have not been conducive to forming a marital relationship. Therefore, I have never married and have no children. I greatly admire and even envy those who are fortunate enough to find a life partner during their early years and then live their lives together as they raise a family. Realistically, if I had married I would never have found the extensive amount of time that I needed to research and write this book. Maybe this is how my life was meant to be. Still, in the midst of a somewhat chaotic life, I am pleased to say that I have enjoyed the friendship of some fine women over the years, and still do.

Here is another personal philosophy that may be of interest: While a few individuals may reach stages of perfection, most of us are simply trying to improve our lives. Somehow and in some way we wish to alleviate our pains and live in greater comfort, physically and emotionally. Many of us still have a long way to go, and that includes this writer. At the same time, along one's pathway through life, I believe that it is appropriate to share with others what one has learned thus far. This is the purpose for this book, to share the few things that I have learned during the first seventy-plus years of my life's journey, with a realization there is still much more to learn. I like to reflect on the sport of archery in which errors are referred to as *sins*, where "sin" is defined as "missing the mark." Many of us are simply trying to get through life and we admittedly make mistakes; in other words there are times when we "miss the mark." Therefore, in a somewhat lighthearted mood, I kindly ask that readers not demean the sinners in this world. We are the majority! We deserve your sympathy and compassion! ☺

341

1. Isabel Briggs Myers, *Gifts Differing: Understanding Personality Type*, with her son Peter B. Myers, CPP, Reprint Edition (Jan. 1995), ISBN-10:089106074X, ISBN-13:978-0891060741

2. David Kiersey, *Please Understand Me: Character and Temperament Types*, coauthored with Marilyn Bates, B & D Books; 5th edition (November 1, 1984), ISBN-10: 0960695400, ISBN-13: 978-0960695409

3. David Kiersey, *Please Understand Me II: Temperament, Character, Intelligence*, Prometheus Nemesis Book Co; 1st Edition (May 1, 1998), ISBN-10: 1885705026, ISBN-13: 978-1885705020

4. Noreen Monroe Guzie and Tad Guzie, *About Men & Women: How Your Masculine and Feminine Archetypes Shape Your Destiny. Understanding Your Personality, Goals, Relationships & Stages of Life. A Complement to the Psychological Types.* Enlightenment Publications, L.L.C.; 2nd edition (June 10, 2016), ISBN-10: 0997204206, ISBN-13: 978-0997204209

5. Brian P. Hall, *The Development of Consciousness—A Confluent Theory of Values*, Paulist Press (1976), ISBN-10: 0809118947, ISBN-13: 978-0809118946

6. Brian P. Hall, *Developing Human Values*, coauthored with Bruce Taylor, Janet Kalvin and Larry S. Rosen, International Values Institute of Marian College (September 1, 1990), ISBN-10: 1879494019, ISBN-13: 978-1879494015

7. Brian P. Hall, *The Genesis Effect—Personal and Organizational Transformations*, Wipf & Stock Pub (August 1, 2006), ISBN-10: 1597527025, ISBN-13: 978-1597527026

8. Brian P. Hall, *Values Shift—A Guide to Personal and Organizational Transformation*, Resource Publications (August 1, 2006), ISBN-10: 1597526908, ISBN-13: 978-1597526906

Manufactured by Amazon.ca
Bolton, ON